Embodied Performativity in Southeast Asia

A collection presenting cutting-edge research from music, dance, performance art, fashion and visual arts, written by scholar-practitioners working in South-East Asia.

This eclectic monograph explores multi-disciplinarily performativity through the body. Exploring the notion of the body as central to creative practice it draws together conversations centring on innovation through embodied knowledge relating to space, time and place. The authors of this collection are leaders in their fields and recognized internationally. Their chapters represent new directions in thought and practice by game-changers in the arts. Underpinned by a central theme of corporeality, it is bold and innovative in its scope and range, bringing diverse disciplines together. It enables connections that create new ways of critically exploring corporeality, extending beyond physicality and the traditional body-centred areas of performing arts practice.

Insightful and stimulating reading for students, scholars and practitioners across the tertiary arts sector as well as education, therapy, cultural studies and inter-disciplinary arts.

Stephanie Burridge (PhD) lectures at LASALLE College of the Arts and Singapore Management University. She was Artistic Director of Canberra Dance Theater (1978–2001) and was awarded the first Fellowship at the Australian Choreographic Center. She has published over 30 academic papers and articles, and is the Series Editor for Routledge *Celebrating Dance in Asia and the Pacific*, commissioning anthologies from Cambodia, India, Malaysia, Australia, Taiwan, Singapore and the South Pacific. Other book series from Routledge are: *Perspectives on Dance, Young People and Change*, which includes *Dance Education around the World* (2015); *Dance Access and Inclusion* (2017); and *Dance Crossing Borders* (2020). She serves on several journal editorial panels and is a choreographer, performer, dance writer, educator and critic.

Routledge Contemporary Southeast Asia Series

The aim of this series is to publish original, high-quality work by both new and established scholars on all aspects of Southeast Asia.

The Political Economy of Growth in Vietnam
Between States and Markets
Guanie Lim

ASEAN and Power in International Relations
ASEAN, the EU, and the Contestation of Human Rights
Jamie D. Stacey

The Army and Ideology in Indonesia
From Dwifungsi to Bela Negara
Muhamad Haripin, Adhi Priamarizki and Keoni Indrabayu Marzuki

The 2018 and 2019 Indonesian Elections
Identity Politics and Regional Perspectives
Edited by Leonard C Sebastian and Alexander R Arifianto

Embodied Performativity in Southeast Asia
Multidisciplinary Corporealities
Edited by Stephanie Burridge

For more information about this series, please visit: www.routledge.com/Routledge-Contemporary-Southeast-Asia-Series/book-series/RCSEA

Embodied Performativity in Southeast Asia

Multidisciplinary Corporealities

Edited by
Stephanie Burridge

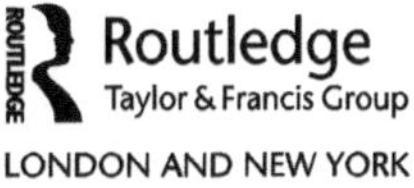

LONDON AND NEW YORK

First published 2021
by Routledge
2 Park Square, Milton Park, Abingdon, Oxon OX14 4RN

and by Routledge
605 Third Avenue, New York, NY 10017

First issued in paperback 2022

Routledge is an imprint of the Taylor & Francis Group, an informa business

British Library Cataloguing-in-Publication Data
A catalogue record for this book is available from the British Library

Library of Congress Cataloging-in-Publication Data
A catalog record has been requested for this book

ISBN: 978-0-367-56755-2 (pbk)
ISBN: 978-0-367-82047-3 (hbk)
ISBN: 978-1-003-01162-0 (ebk)

DOI: 10.4324/9781003011620

Typeset in Times New Roman
by codeMantra

Contents

Figures

Contributors

Glenna Batson (PT, ScD.) is an independent lecturer, researcher, mentor and performer. For over four decades, she has honed a trans-disciplinary approach to the study of embodiment, bridging between dance, science, phenomenology and somatic studies. Glenna is professor emeritus of physical therapy at Winston-Salem State University (USA) and an internationally recognised teacher of the Alexander Technique. Practice-based research includes *Human Origami*, an improvisation on the biological archive of bodily folding, and dancing while aging. Author of *Body and Mind in Motion: Dance and Neuroscience in Conversation* and co-editor/contributor to *Dance, Somatics and Spiritualities: Contemporary Sacred Narratives.*

Romanian-born and London-trained, fashion designer **Dinu C.T. Bodiciu** received his Master's degree in Fashion Design and Technology at London College of Fashion. His graduation collection, presented at the Victoria and Albert Museum, drew media attention with its shapes, textures and styling. Informed by his work experience in theatre, which spanned over ten years, Dinu creates designs that play with volumes, organic textures and visceral colours in order to alter our perception of the human body. Dinu's biggest celebrity moment came when Lady Gaga wore one of his designs on *The Tonight Show with Jay Leno.* His work has also been showcased in established fashion magazines, such as Vogue, Vision China, Bazaar Asia, Elle and L'Officiel Ukraine.

Elizabeth de Roza (PhD) is Senior Lecturer in the School of Dance and Theatre at LASALLE College of the Arts, Singapore. She co-convenes the Embodied Research Working Group within the International Federation for Theatre Research and also serves as an Assistant Editor for the Journal of Embodied Research. Elizabeth is internationally known as an artist-scholar, performance maker, theatre director, actor-movement trainer. Elizabeth's research interests focus on embodied experiences, thinking and practice through making, embodied cognition and cross-cultural performance at the intersections of both decolonial and feminist theories. She holds a PhD (Theatre and Performance) from Goldsmiths, University of London.

Darren Moore (PhD) is a drummer, electronic musician and academic working in the fields of jazz, electronic music, experimental music and multi-media throughout South-East Asia, Australia, Japan and Europe. Since 2006, he has been a Lecturer in Music at LASALLE College of the Arts, Singapore. His Doctorate of Musical Arts was completed at Griffith University in 2013 and looked at the adaptation of Carnatic Indian rhythms to the drum set. His research interests centre on drum set improvisatory practice on drum set and modular synthesiser.

Timothy O'Dwyer (PhD) is an Australian saxophonist, improviser and composer, who has been a lecturer and Head of the School of Contemporary Music at LASALLE College of the Arts, Singapore, since 2004. Over the past 25 years, Tim has been a prolific performer and collaborator, traversing jazz, improvised and experimental electro-acoustic music, contemporary classical music and cross-disciplinary projects. He regularly performs with the leading contemporary musicians of our time in Europe, Asia and Australia with ELISION Ensemble (since 1994), The Australian Art Orchestra and many groups led by himself and in collaboration with others. His research interests involve integrating the concepts of Gilles Deleuze with his creative practice, critical reflections on the live composing practice of 'soundpainting' and the pedagogy of improvised music.

Shelly Quick is a theatre director and multi-disciplinary artist. Her work examines the intersection of artistic disciplines and the performativity of objects, images and lived-in spaces. Past works include the immersive, site-responsive *Lower Depths: 61 Kerbau Road* (Singapore); performance installations *Paper Boat* and *The Wedding Guest's Tale* (Canada and Singapore); and, most recently, *Ephemera Etc*, a photographic response to Fundacio Vila Casas's collection of paintings in Barcelona's museum Can Framis (Barcelona).

Susan Sentler is a dance artist working as teacher, choreographer, researcher, director and performer. She served as senior lecturer with

Trinity Laban Conservatoire of Music and Dance for 18 years and has taught globally in the field of dance for over 30 years. Susan's creative practice is multi-disciplinary, anchored by a honed somatic relationship to image. She works in gallery/museum contexts, creating 'responses' or 'activations' within exhibitions as well as durational installations orchestrating objects, sound, moving/still image and absence/presence of the performing body. Her work has been exhibited and performed in the UK, the USA, Europe and Singapore. She is a lecturer in the School of Dance & Theatre at LASALLE College of the Arts, Singapore.

Clare Veal (PhD) is a lecturer in the MA Asian Art Histories programme at LASALLE College of the Arts, Singapore. She received her PhD from the Department of Art History and Film Studies at the University of Sydney and undertakes research on South-East Asian photography, art and visual culture, with a particular focus on Thailand and questions of sexual difference, subjectivity and agency. Clare has contributed papers to publications, including *Journal of Aesthetics and Culture*, *Afterall* and *Trans-Asia Photography Review*. She is currently an editorial collective member for *Southeast of Now: Directions in Contemporary and Modern Art in Asia* and is a founding co-member of the Gender in Southeast Asian Art Research Network.

Acknowledgements

This volume arose from a research seminar series at LASALLE College of the Arts, Singapore. I extend thanks and gratitude to the college and, in particular, Dr Wolfgang Muench, Dean, Learning, Teaching & Research, for his support of this inter-disciplinary research endeavour and his encouragement of its publication.

The editor would like to acknowledge the outstanding contributions that the authors have made to this book. I want to thank Routledge for their foresight in commissioning this volume and their understanding of the complexity of assembling such a rich and diverse collection of authors for the anthology.

Introduction

Stephanie Burridge

This eclectic monograph investigates corporealities across diverse arts practices – dance, music, fashion, visual and performance art. The six chapters resulted from a multidisciplinary seminar series at LASALLE College of the Arts, a tertiary arts institution in Singapore – the unifying themes were the body, embodied performativity and multidisciplinarity. This research series on what initially appear to be disparate titles was curated to facilitate dialogues about the notion of the body as central to all creative practice, with an objective to enable and enhance inter-disciplinary relationships and pedagogy. *Corporeality – the body as central to artmaking and the creative process* included three presentations from dance and contemporary music practitioners, while *Transcultural hybridity – investigating embodied interdisciplinary creative languages,* the second session, introduced a performance artist, a fashion designer and a curator/historian of visual culture. The six teaching artists came together to not only present their current research but participate in robust discussions about the scope of the words 'corporealities' and 'embodiment'. All acknowledged a plurality of meanings that extended beyond the physical, culturally contextualized body to explorations of mind/body connections: somatic and visceral experiences expressed through movement and gesture. Although each artist's research was presented as a discrete study with specific case examples and outcomes, an underlying intention was to find commonalities and linkages between them. Theoretical framing and methods, along with performative workshops and performance/exhibition descriptors, flowed across the topic areas and aligned creative practice and the body. Modelling of cross-disciplinary pedagogies and opportunities to extend artistic boundaries of collaboration emerged.

South-East Asian focus

The research was centred in Singapore, with outreach projects, workshops and performance events in other selected Asian countries (Thailand and Myanmar) as well as Australia, the UK and Germany. Representations of the body materialised across multiple planes, including immersive, experiential and reflective domains. Conversations about creation processes through embodied knowledge relating to space, time and place support the critical analysis in these essays. The South-East Asian context of cultural traditions; ritual; and symbolism, metaphors and imagery often gave a sense of a journey; this narrative was a recurring theme, essentialising the performative practice as the artists mapped responses to the same work as it travelled to different countries. All sought collaborations and performative opportunities and inspiration as these transitional journeys became embedded in their practice. These trajectories are documented in the research chapters; for example, observations of Javanese Wayang shadow puppets inspired a new direction in contemporary fashion by incorporating the image of an extended body by including the shadow.

A sense of place, cultural memories and embodied ways of thinking and moving emerged as new audiences, and participants, engaged with each project. Charting and recording these variations are central to comprehending the impact of art as it crosses borders – geographical, cultural, social and educational, among others. The liminal spaces existing between the artist and the audience, the teacher and the participants, the creator and the wearer, become illuminated zones of experience, incorporating action and reflection. In these shifting cultural contexts viewers are challenged to respond using their own embodied knowledge via immersion, improvisation, listening, experiencing, touching and viewing.

Materiality also featured as a connection in several chapters. Paper – as folded material echoing traditional Japanese origami, paper boats carrying memories and folded pattern making material – juxtaposed a simple craft redolent with tactile childhood memories with complex ritual and spirituality. Disrupting the simplicity of this source of inspiration is the use of current techniques in neurobiology to power a contemporary synthesizer, as outlined in the last chapter of this volume. Metal and jumbled wiring clash, driven by biological human tissue – here the mechanics of bodily function united with medical technology give rise to potentialities that seem to blur the edges of embodiment as a central creative impetus.

The body in death polarizes movement and stillness yet invites agency for reflection, memories, thoughts and feelings, linking, in the case of the artwork in this volume, the sculptural artefact with the viewer. This matrix of existential reality reverberates into threshold areas with the body as a responsive, evocative site, engaging with the subliminal, stored memory fields; dreams; archival traces; and the mundane.

Theoretical framing

The historiography of the body (Foucault, 1972) thematically layers contexts resulting in a transcultural hybridity with multiple creative languages and inflections – a site for spontaneous body expression and improvisation (Sheets-Johnstone, 2011). This seminar series foregrounded personal interpretation of symbol systems and nuances across softening borders of disciplines as the researchers sought to create and align practice through a theoretical lens, sometimes as a tool for inspiration or for reflection and clarification.

While the artists acknowledge the theories of scholars across their discrete fields, the common interest in the French phenomenologist Maurice Merleau-Ponty (2001) and post-structuralist Gilles Deleuze (1993) emerged as a shared thread: the first for uniting the essential notions of embodiment with phenomenology; the second for the idea of transformation and 'becoming'. More directly for this volume the image of the Deleuzian 'fold' is critiqued in two chapters, one on dance and another on sound – both directly named this as their sustaining direction.

Pedagogy

Transference from an original idea into a working method to enable sharing to students is a concern in most chapters. Several projects narrated in the volume included tertiary-level student involvement, while others adopted reflective practices not only on the creative process and outcomes but also on how these might impact and influence student teaching and learning. Juxtapositions across these stratifications threw up fresh perspectives, approaches and actualizations in a mesh of pathways and cross-reference points. Some ideas, for example, including the shadow as part of body image in design, are clearly translated into a method that can be implemented as an experimental option for fashion students; other image-based work, like that incorporating the idea of a fold in dance or a paper boat carrying memories, open up spaces for individual interpretation and expression.

Other ideas, such as student's immersion to tease out philosophical strands, work on a conceptual level that encourages deeper critical analysis and evaluation for students. The summary below introduces the concepts and practice in the chapters in this book.

Chapter summary

Performance artists **Elizabeth de Roza** and **Shelly Quick** take their project to three continents to explore the body, cultural specificity and audience engagement in *Paper Boats*. Here the body is present as a performative springboard for audience participation as they move together, creating and recreating memories. This transaction of the embodied self is facilitated through storytelling and the use of simple props that enable a ritualistic flow and transcend time in various ways. The ceremonial burning of the paper boats in the final performance is both a cathartic dissimulation of all the shared memories and a sense of closure as metaphors abound.

Contemporary musician **Timothy O'Dwyer** discusses a project as a manifestation of incorporeal and corporeal events using Leibniz's Psychic Geometry, Musical Monads and other conceptual trajectories found in Deleuze's *The Fold: Leibniz and the Baroque*. Staged in Singapore and Cologne, *The Fold* is a collaborative composing project involving musicians from disparate cultural and stylistic backgrounds. The musicians came together to compose written scores that were then used for improvisation during their performances. Musical monads and other conceptual trajectories found in Deleuze's *The Fold: Leibniz and the Baroque* are incorporated (1993).

Dancer/choreographer and educator **Susan Sentler** works with somatic specialist **Glenna Batson** to devise body imagery also aligned to Deleuzian theory of the fold as image-based practice. Designed to enhance conservatory dancers' perception and attention to the dynamics of bodily folding, the improvisational structures give rise to an embodied ontology of *becoming* whose unfixed boundaries are iterative, non-linear and liminal. The multiplicity of movement patterns emerging from folding give way to a fractal field of potential which can redefine bodily dimensionality.

Fashion designer **Dinu Bodiciu** problematizes the conventional methods in fashion's approach to the body as a subject to be dressed. By expanding the borders of the body into the territory of the two dimensionality of shadows (inspired by Javanese Wayang puppets) he notes the potential to dissolve perceptions of race, size, individuality, gender and identity. Under the influence of light, transient features or shadows that the body produces onto surrounding surfaces can be considered impalpable extensions which trace our existence and continuously accompany us.

Art historian and curator **Clare Veal** examines the early sculptural and installation practices of renowned Thai artist and writer Araya Rasdjarmrearnsook (b. 1957) from an intermedial perspective, articulating how the production and reception of her sculptures and installations involve an interplay between moving and static bodies. Felt experiences, contemplative and reflective zones of incubation, have transformative congruency to receptive viewers who might engage with the work culturally, politically or antithetically.

Finally, **Darren Moore** moves into new territory, creating an artwork that embodies biological material with a musical body, using cultured in-vitro human neurons as the engine to drive a custom-made analogue modular synthesiser. cellF is the world's first neuron-driven synthesiser. It is a collaborative project at the cutting edge of experimental art and music that brings together artists, musicians, designers and scientists to create a cybernetic musical entity. *cellF* is an autonomous, bioanalogue electronic musical instrument designed to operate independently and interact with human musicians.

Embodied performativity

American philosopher Sheets-Johnstone states, 'As one might wonder about the world in words, I am wondering the world directly, in movement' (Sheets-Johnstone, 2011, p. 422), while Indian dancer/choreographer/activist Chandralekha's life's work was the interrogation of the body – the feminist body; the sexual, political, the creative and resistant body. She states, 'My concern is with the body… where does it begin…where does it end?' (Chandralekha, 2014). The essence is the connection of the embodied self, expressed through movement, relating to the world.

Similarly, the research in this volume admits investigation through lived experiences transcending the essentialised notion of a physical being and moving towards a convergence of the biological body and somatic, visceral comprehension. Centralising the body as a 'site of perception' and experience (Dewey, 1934; Shusterman, 2013) enables shared traces, relics or artefacts to exist in moments of time; here improvisation might be a fleeting ephemeral moment, while a sculpture, musical composition or garment have different permanence. This multidisciplinary corporeality offers insights across art-making perspectives and enables myriad entry points to creativity, from whole body framing to gestural impulses, meditation, improvisation and play.

This 'soft landing' for the imagination is in stark contrast to the voices of disrupters who seek to negotiate the proposition of the body via new technologies, biomechanics and augmented realities. Artists such as Stelarc (1991) celebrate possibilities that negate an elevated platform for the body by articulating its limitations. The ontology of the body comes into question as artists augment its boundaries utilising prosthetics, tissue art and transgenic art (O'Donnell, 2011).

Unifying the essays in this monograph is the body… and it invites a response. The six essays reposition the corporealities and challenge parameters through embodied performativity across diverse disciplines. Biological function; extrinsic illumination through shadows; poetics evoking memory fields as a depository for embodied meaning; and cultural specificity through time, space and place collide – the possibilities flow in a continuum.

References

Deleuze, Gilles. (1993). *The Fold: Leibnitz and the Baroque.* Minneapolis, MN: Regents of the University of Minnesota.

Dewey, John. (1934). *Art as Experience*, reprinted in 1989, *John Dewey: The Later Works, 1925–1953*, vol. 10. (ed. J. Boydston). Carbondale: Southern Illinois University Press.

Foucault, Micheal. (1972). *The Archeology of Knowledge.* (trans. A.M. Sheridan Smith). New York: Pantheon.

Merleau-Ponty, Maurice. (2001). *Phenomenology of Perception [Phénoménologie de la perception].* Routledge & Kegan Paul (First Published 1954).

O'Donnell, Ryan P. (2011). 'Posthuman: Exploring the Obsolescence of the Corporeal Body in Contemporary Art', *Inquiries*, Vol. 3, No. 8,pp. 1/1. http://www.inquiriesjournal.com/articles/564/posthuman-exploring-the-obsolescence-of-the-corporeal-body-in-contemporary-art (accessed April 5, 2019).

Sheets-Johnstone, Maxine. (2011). *The Primacy of Movement: Advances in Consciousness Research.* Amsterdam/Philadelphia, PA: John Benjamin Publishing Company.

Shusterman, Richard. (2013). 'Body and the Arts: The Need for Somaesthetics', *SAGE Journals*, https://doi.org/10.1177/0392192112469159.

Stelarc. (1991) 'Prosthetics, Robotics and Remote Existence: Postrevolutionary Strategies', *Leonardo*, Vol. 24, No. 5, pp. 591–595. https://www.jstor.org/stable/1575667?seq=1#page_scan_tab_contents (accessed May 7, 2019).

Sharira – Chandralekha's Explorations in Dance. (2014) Directed by Ein Lall; Producer & Commissioning Editor – Rajiv Mehrotra, PSBT India. https://www.youtube.com/watch?v=vyXh_5dT0zw (accessed April 5, 2019).

1 Case study: *Paper Boat* – an embodied response to sites/ places and memories

(Myanmar, Singapore and Germany)

Elizabeth de Roza and Shelly Quick

Introduction

This co-authored practitioner narrative chapter articulates both the process and the performance of *Paper Boat*, highlighting an experiential encounter of how it was conceived and how the performance was received. The chapter is written in two voices, namely Shelly Quick (SQ) as the dramaturge and co-performer, and Elizabeth de Roza (EdR) as co-creator and performer, with additional text (in italics) from a reflection by another performer, Oon Shu An, as input towards the performance text. Through the writing, we hope to create a shared embodied experience for the reader.

About the process

SQ

The day that *Paper Boat* began was a Saturday. The year was 2008. Elizabeth de Roza stood in the rehearsal space, barefooted and negotiating a path through some 50 paper boats she had folded and placed around her feet. The trajectory she took followed an invisible line, a line of memory that traced back to her childhood and the drains, now covered, that she used to float paper boats in after the monsoon rains. I watched her, noting her trajectory, projecting my own story onto the site of her body, finding the bones of the physical score we would travel with.

It is important to be specific about the site of origin of *Paper Boat* because, when we were first creating the work, we were in a city-state where the original sites of so many of our experiences were disappearing. Memory was under siege. Beloved buildings were being torn down at an alarming rate. Whole neighbourhoods were disappearing. If we left the city for a few months, we could come back and lose our way. Not that we needed to orient ourselves to navigate the island. The island itself, with its spidering systems of transport, now whizzed us from one place to another, mostly underground, so that we no longer needed to know where we were between points of departing and arriving.

The architect Juhani Pallasmaa has remarked that 'along with the entire corpus of literature and the arts, landscapes and buildings constitute the most important externalization of human memory' (Pallasmaa, 2009, p. 17). He also observes that

> With the dizzying acceleration of the velocity of time today and the constant speeding up of our experiential reality, we are seriously threatened by a general cultural amnesia. In today's accelerated life we can ultimately only perceive, not remember. In the society of the spectacle we can only marvel, not remember.
>
> (Pallasmaa, 2009, p. 32)

Living in Singapore felt like living Pallasmaa's academic discourse. Our daily lives embodied it.

SQ

Spurred on by our personal experiences and Pallasmaa's essay, we decided to create a rupture in accelerated time, to take back slowness and stillness, and to create a space for our audience to be still and remember. *Paper Boat* was our rebellion, our attempt to disrupt the speed of forgetting – to tear a hole in the veil falling between what we saw in our mind's eye, what our bodies remembered and what had disappeared.

The philosopher Edward S. Casey argues that 'there is no memory without body memory' (Casey, 2000, p. 172). So, *Paper Boat* began in the body, the body of Elizabeth de Roza and her memories.

EdR

The first impulse for me came from this innate memory of the sensation I had as a child when I first played with a paper boat – the association of a memory that I had forgotten came back in waves through my body.

The sound of the rain became audible, the sensation of how my body felt when I stood by the monsoon drain and watched how the paper boat floated on the water and disappeared as the current led the boat away. Slowly my body started creating this inner rhythm; the rhythm came from my breathing pattern, and with each inhalation, I found a way through my body in this: a state of quietude and a profound sense of stillness that was within and then into this heart[1] of experience in which I could restore this emotional atmosphere.

Carrying this profound sense of stillness within me, I made my way through the paper boats laid out on the floor of the rehearsal studio – it became, for me, a path of remembering; the act of moving through the boats created an association of moving through a sea of memories, at times tumultuous and at times calming. Simultaneously, whilst moving, I picked up a small paper boat and held it in my palm, and the action of rocking began to emulate the rocking motion of the sea, negotiating a safe passage through for the small boat. And as I moved through the space, I turned to see what was left behind.

The act of looking behind and yet being pulled forward became, for us, the core structure of the work and raised questions for us as we worked through how we would negotiate the creation process and whether *Paper Boat*, as a metaphor for remembering, could be the object of recalling and, as this site of negotiation, a hybrid place in which to graft, to interweave, the site and culture of the country that was hosting us.

SQ

When we first began to create *Paper Boat*, we had no idea where we would take the performance, but we sensed that our experiences in Singapore were shared in cities all over the world. Although there were variations in tempi throughout the work, slowness dominated: it was a strategy. Like the flaneurs of 19th-century Paris, who walked their tortoises through the arcades in deliberate opposition to the increasing speed of their city, we developed a deliberately slow-moving performance, with actions and images fading, almost imperceptibly, into each other. The work was without dialogue, the sound atmospheric and without tempo. Our aim was to situate the viewer in their own world, the actors' bodies and the mise en scène acting as a site of collective imagining and remembering.

Over the next six years, the performance travelled to five different countries, all moving at different speeds of experiential reality. And it became our challenge to find a way to create and recreate a site for collective imagining and remembering in each of the places we performed. It would be impossible to discuss each performance in detail in this chapter, so we will discuss only three: our first performance, which took place in Myanmar; our second performance, which took place in Singapore; and our final performance in Berlin.

About the performances

Myanmar

In Myanmar, *Paper Boat* was part of a festival unsanctioned by the government. Technically it took place on French soil rather than Myanmar's as it operated on the grounds of the Alliance Francaise, which enjoyed the privileges of diplomatic immunity. We arrived some ten days before the performance; in addition to performing *Paper Boat,* we trained a group of young Myanmar actors and developed a work with them that they performed for the festival. This training was key to how *Paper Boat* took shape in the city of Yangon. Our daily interactions with the young actors and other Myanmar performers influenced how we situated the movement score and designed the mise en scène. We would work with the actors during the day and develop *Paper Boat* in the evening. We had brought the work to the festival in a state that was deliberately unfinished so there was room in it for the community we would perform for, as well as the site of the performance itself, to have a hand in its final shape.

Through our work with the young actors, we began to realise that while we were interested in looking back, or staying still, our audience could very well be more interested in looking forward. We decided to make paper boats with the audience members before the performance began and to encourage them to write their hopes, fears, dreams and memories on them. Our young students helped us to speak to the audience members before the performance and to make paper boats with them. This pre-show interaction with the audience is something we came to consider a part of the performance itself. When it was time for the section of the performance we had choreographed and loosely designed, we invited the audience into the performance space: a conference hall in the Alliance Francaise. Each member of the audience entered clutching a paper boat.

EdR

In silence, I entered the space from the back of the audience, with my eyes downcast and my palms opened. There was this sense of urgency as I walked through the audience space as each audience member made it a point to give me their boats of desires; these boats of memories and desires were placed on my palms, and then I put them in my pockets – if any boats fell out of my pockets the audience would somehow pick them up and put them back into my palm. There was this sense of a charged and shared energy in the space, and everyone wanted to ensure that the boats were passed to me (Figure 1.1).

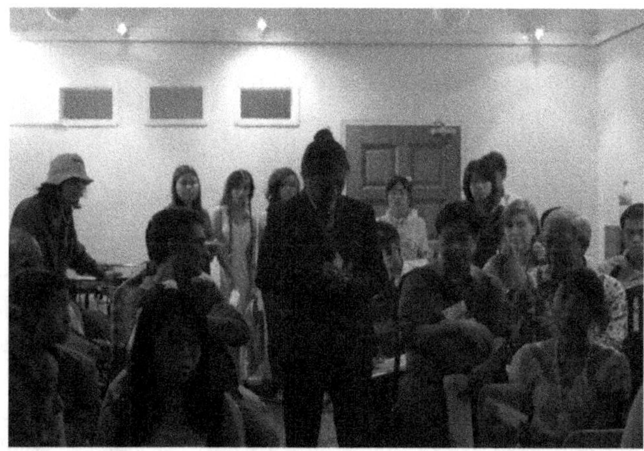

Figure 1.1 Myanmar (audience handing out paper boats to performer Elizabeth de Roza). Courtesy of the artists.

EdR continues

I arrived at the edge of between the audience space and the performing space; I turned around and looked back at the audience and then carried their boats of desires across; the act of 'carry-across' became a 'crossing-over' and transformed these desires into a projection of a manifestation of hope. As I carried the boats across, a new space was opened, and this became a shared space for both the audience and me. Through their writing, the audience had their voices interwoven into the performance. The paper boats I had in my pockets became charged objects of interaction, a currency for a kind of transaction between me, the performer, the guest and host in this liminal space of neither Myanmar nor France, neither my territory nor theirs, and the audience, who were also guests and hosts to the performance.

The process of opening a shared space in this area of uncertain boundaries created a simultaneous embodied reflection for me. I endeavoured to remain open, to create a genuinely responsive and contemplative space within the evolving choreographic score of the pre-existing structure of 'looking back and being pulled forward'. The physical score and the co-produced mise en scène created through the placement of the audience's handmade paper boats and writings became a space for cross-cultural encounters. The hybrid of cross-cultural encounters happened because of the varied cultural dimensions of the audience and me, and represented a very brief but charged exchange through the sharing of writings in the handing over of the paper boats and crossing over into the performance space. The 'affect' of this emphasised a phenomenological dimension of the lived experience of the audience as they entrusted me with their desires through the handing over of paper boats.

SQ

At the close of the performance, many audience members cried. They immediately approached us, filling the space where the performance had been enacted, asking about their boats, wondering where they had been placed and what would happen to them next. This material artefact of the performance was something we had not planned for in our original designing of the work. Perhaps because we were accustomed to the common practice of dispensing with any set pieces created for a work after our performances, we had failed to think about what we would do with these fragments of hopes, dreams and memories offered to us by our audience. With the help of our actor-students, we gathered up all the boats, making the decision to bring them with us to the next performance, wherever that would be, using them as a first phase of the next mise en scène.

After the performance in Myanmar, we had the opportunity to perform the work in Singapore as part of Esplanade Theatre Studio Series *Closer*. Although we had received positive feedback from our audience in Myanmar, we questioned the interactive element of the work. There had been a shared space and a place for the voices of the audience in the work, but we wanted to expand it. We wondered how we could re-shape it to give the viewers more of a voice in the performance. Also, whereas in Myanmar the site of the performance had been intimate, lacking the trappings of a formal performance space, we would now be working in a black box in the Esplanade-Theatres at the Bay, a large performing arts centre in Singapore's downtown core (Figure 1.2).

Singapore

SQ continues

We proposed to the Esplanade that we place a large cargo box in its concourse. The box could be entered, and inside there was a small table, two chairs, a carpet and a recording device. Our plan, as a pre-performance activity, was to use the cargo box as a kind of 'confessional booth'. The public passing through were invited to confess their hopes, dreams,

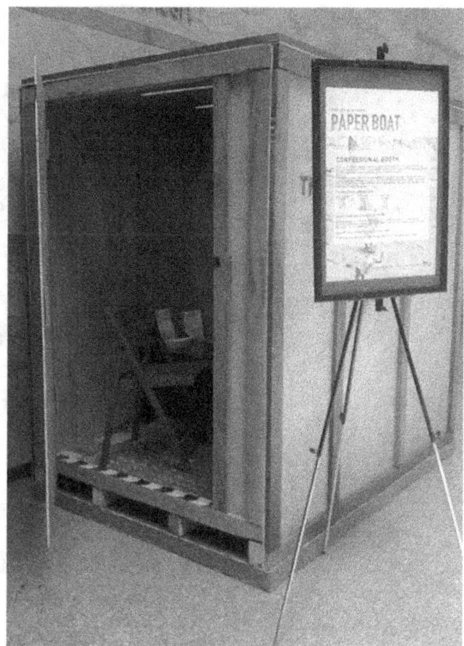

Figure 1.2 Confessional booth at the Esplanade (Singapore). Courtesy of the artists.

fears, regrets, disappointments and memories, either to one of us (who was always with the booth) or to the recording device. The Esplanade agreed to the plan, and we set up the booth a month before the performance. With the participants' permission, the recorded statements became the soundscape of performance in the black box. As we listened to the recordings over the days leading up to the black box portion of the work, we redesigned the physical score, keeping key movement motifs and gestures but also adding new ones, lengthening the shape and duration of some of the movements and truncating others (Figure 1.3).

EdR

My first impulse was to listen, and so I began the work in the rehearsal studio by first standing still and listening. As I stood still to listen, I worked with my breath, and with each inhalation, I sensed this moment of a held-thought that gave shape to a physical action that was

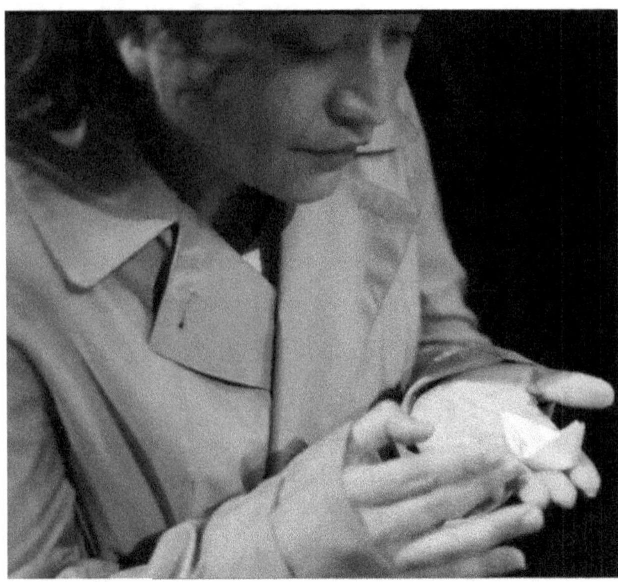

Figure 1.3 Performer Elizabeth de Roza cradling a small paper boat at the performance in Esplanade (Singapore).

translated through my body as a kind vibrational memory. This vibrational memory took shape through my body, through tiny gestures/physical actions.

This time, the tiny boat that I carried in my palm became, for me, the fragility of the collective memory that was shared in Myanmar. The rocking action of my body seeped from deep within my embodied recalling of the charged atmosphere needed to find its own space, and so rather than showing the recalling, my body became this site of non-action – an act of rebellion towards the need for a showing. My body needed to be still, to invite the audience to come in – to draw the audience in so that they could be in this space with me, and for them to listen intently and reflect inwardly. At this moment, we decided that we would develop an even deeper slowness as an integral element of the performance to create this probing reflection process and to create this atmosphere of soul-searching and inviting the audience to turn inwards.

It was important for us to create this sensation/feeling of a lived experience rather than an anecdote. Perhaps the sensation of this lived experience might seem rather elusive, but if these sensations come into contact with the body and trigger an association, these associations become concrete; the trajectory of the route of recalling and sharing becomes more precise; and the body can lead these associations to draw the essence of its presence and its shape, and affect the experience of the audience. These triggers initiate a process of remembering and are a phenomenology of imagination (Bachelard, 1958) that emerges from an intimate immense experience through the body. The body is herself a site of acknowledgement, and through the body we can experience things. The body stands amongst things in the world. It has a point of view through which it sees things (Bachelard, 1958; Merleau-Ponty, 2001; Shusterman, 2012). The body is marked by her experiences because within a site of action, there is liveness. This liveness is the body's response to the experiences that she encapsulates. Through these experiences, the body makes sense of how she is affected and comprehends what is happening around her.

SQ

With the investment of time, and a deliberate looseness to the shape of our work, we were attempting to create an interactive, transactional collaboration with the community we were making the work for. We were feeling our way to a place where we could collectively shape the landscape of the performance. We aspired to treat our work like a living thing, something that was sensitive to its environment yet sturdy enough to be grafted onto, to change shape but not species, through its interaction with the audience community.

In addition to the community and cultures we encountered in our pre-show confessional booth, there were other cultures we were working with at the Esplanade. There was the unseen but ever-present community of a formal, structured performance space. Many of the rules and regulations, as well as conventions and norms, of the space worked against our desire for looseness and creating and responding in the moment. There was an expectation that elements of mise en scène be set, lighting plotted, sound pre-designed. We could take out the raked seating but had to design a plan in its place. We would have a technical team. A certain level of aesthetic value had to be met – even our cargo box had to meet these expectations: the wood had to be finished, the font of the lettering on its side approved, before it could be placed in the foyer.

Feeling this unseen pressure, we put more craft into our scenography. We had a large boat built and hung others, with small lights in them, over the performance space. Our boats from Myanmar traced a line across the floor, pre-set and unmoving. We employed sound and video designers to work with pre-recorded and live materials so that the audience experienced time in multiple layers, both through their own memories and through their lived experience in the performance. We also added a second actor to the performance.

EdR

We made the deliberate decision to collaborate with another, younger performer (Oon Shu An) because we wanted to create a juxtaposition of personal narratives and see how a younger person would respond to her own set memories, her(his)tory.

Together we worked in the studio, asking the following questions:

1 What is the history of your/our body and the environment that your/our body is exposed to?
2 What is the negotiation of what seems to be happening internally and what you think is happening in the space?
3 What is this inner dialogue that is created – and what memories surface?

In asking these questions, we wanted to create an emergence of a human individual space[2] that begins the process of allowing the individual embodied silence to be heard (Figure 1.4).

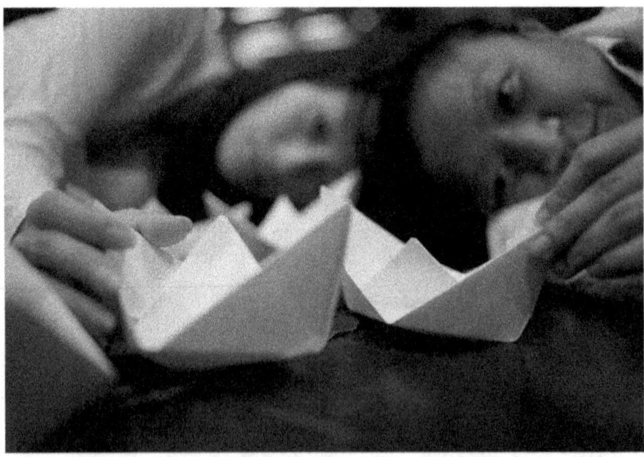

Figure 1.4 Performers Elizabeth de Roza and Oon Shu An in rehearsals. Courtesy of the artists.

What was interesting was that Shu An did not have a close association with paper boats. In fact, the idea of making a paper boat or playing with them was foreign to her. Instead of imposing a foreign object onto her, I asked what objects she could closely relate to. This is was her reply:

> The strange thing about places in our lives, objects, even people, is how we can never predict what's going to be important. Now I try to keep everything just in case. It's very hard to throw away things. I have so many of my old scripts, clothes that I used to wear, letters, stuffed toys, jewelry I bought when I was going through a phase, movie tickets, a flower from someone special, receipts, a bottle of dried up nail polish for reference when I replace it because this line doesn't make that colour anymore – the list goes on – but there just isn't enough space for everything. Walking into my room depresses me because everything is everywhere, it's like a flood of memories that mean nothing in particular, but everything in their possible absence. Even worse, I find myself buying things to replace what I remember having, objects that reminded me of something else. Nothing seems to be what it is in my life; everything has become a representation of what there was or what there might be. I can't move on. I feel like there isn't enough space for the future.

EdR

We began to create an exchange of remembering and memory slowly. The exchange was gestured as an inner action and responded from the elasticity of a muscular reaction. These exchanges, then created a subtle, intimate response of the breath. Interestingly, this intimate, subtle response created an image of destruction and violence for Shu An. The physical action of violently striking her stomach gained an association with the need to make space for new memories, and her memories were various objectifications of her state of mind. This action of destruction became the construction of the creative space through which we were both able to access our embodied memory and share a lived experience.

SQ and EdR

Despite, or possibly because of, the time and money we had to work with in Singapore, when we assessed the work after the run, we felt that an authentic interaction between ourselves and our audience was missed. The cross-cultural encounters, the potentially transformative power of the work, had not been fully realized. We had tried to slow time, to create space in our process and performance for an exchange, a transaction between guest/host/guest, but we had filled too much of the space with the stuff of performance. It came to be our opinion that the most successful element of the performance had been the month-long attendance of our 'confessional booth' and the interactions we had had with the general public passing through the arts complex.

Berlin

EdR

Our final performance of *Paper Boat* was in Berlin. We re-examined our aims for the work and asked ourselves how to connect authentically with the city we were to perform in. This time the performance was part of another exhibition, and we decided on a durational performance.

We managed to spend ten days in Berlin prior to the performance. We walked the city with a translator, trying to learn and allowing ourselves the time and space to encounter the city. Although we had needed translators in Myanmar, and many of the languages of our soundscape in Singapore also had to be translated for us, we felt more linguistically alienated in Germany. This is possibly because we were not situated in one place, encountering people within one section of the city, but rather moving through the city, looking for people to interact with.

We had our translator bring us to the older part of Berlin as we wanted to meet long-time Berliners. In an area of shared allotments, we met a group of older Berliners who had been teachers in East Berlin when the wall was up. With the help of our translator, stories were shared and recorded, but somehow our voice recorder didn't record the stories, and they got lost. This erasure became a departure point for us – and we decided to look at it as a metaphor for the state of being lost in translation/transmission. We wanted to make our inability to speak the language of the country visible and for the audience to consider our position outside the language as part of the shared culture of our performance space. Consequently, Shelly became part of the performance, reading from a German grammar book.

SQ

For this work we had created an environment with paper boats in a large warehouse. The soundscape of pre-recorded interviews with people in Berlin speaking German played over the original soundscape we had used in Myanmar. In one section of the warehouse, I sat reading declensions of verbs, trying to select the verbs most valuable to a beginning speaker of a new language. I chose the verbs to be, to have, to do, to want and to need. I read them subject to verb, through the tenses. We were still talking about time, still talking about experience, but as an alien to a new land, some kind of migrant in a foreign city, untethered from physical history or memory, unable to grasp what had been there not because of disappearance but because of absence. This crossing over, for me, from invisible co-designer and dramaturge to performer, was an important step in finding an authentic exchange and connection between the performance and our audience. The erasure of our recording had ironically led us to struggle to understand and connect visibly within the shared space of the performance (Figure 1.5).

EdR continues

In another part of the warehouse, I invited the audience to tie the strings to the boats and whispered into their ears. The act of whispering into

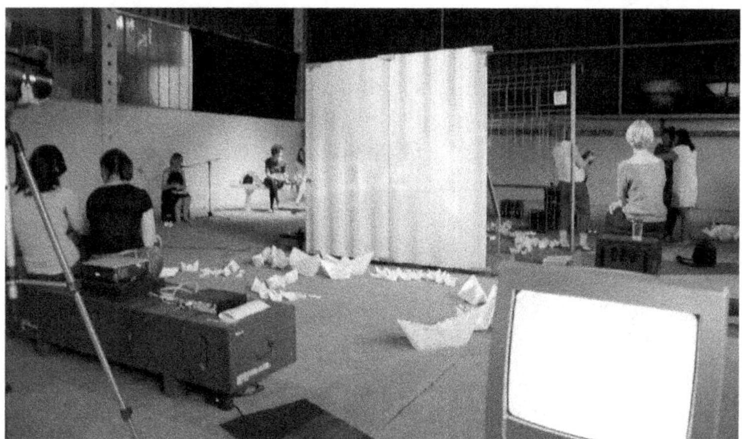

Figure 1.5 Performance in Berlin with Shelly Quick on the left (of the picture) and Elizabeth de Roza on the right (of the picture). Courtesy of the artists.

their ears provided me with the opportunity to be intimate with them as we had learned from the performance in Singapore that *Paper Boats* needed this intimacy.

Slowly, one by one, I would invite and whisper into the viewers' ears; this time, I shared my desires and dreams, and invited them to whisper their dreams and desires to the paper boats scattered on the floor and attach a string to any of the paper boats, which were all connected by a long, red string that was tied to my ankle.

When the piece had reached its conclusion, I left the performance space and set the paper boats on fire, still with the red string attached to my ankle. This was another way to solve the problem of what to do with the boats and pulled the work closer to the realm of ritual, which had perhaps been part of our unspoken intention from the beginning.

Conclusion

In conclusion, the evolving process of creating *Paper Boat* as described was, for both of us, a process of going beyond the forms of artistic expression(s) to create an embodied reflection. With each cross-cultural encounter, we needed to create different possibilities, demonstrating for us the necessity for such performances to continuously evolve in response to the environment in which they are performed. Our performances became a territory of hybridity, a space of guest/host/guest – of foreigner and resident, of individual and collective. Each host city represented, to quote Aldo Rossi, an Italian architect (1931–1997), 'the collective memory of its people, and like memory it (was) associated with objects and places and that the interactive element' (1982, p. 130). We added to the interactive element through our embodied responses and reflections on the environment in which we created and re-created our work.

Notes

1 The heart of experience is central to Heidegger's (2010) notion of thought, which he relates to the experience of understanding and indicating that understanding is existentially situated.
2 By space I mean the site of representation and systems of receptions and perceiving. These sites and systems provide an inward gaze into the human psyche that consists of the imaginary, the symbolic and the real (Lacan).

References

Bachelard, G. (1958) *The Poetics of Space*. The classic look at how we experience intimate places. Boston, MA: Beacon Press Book.

Casey, E. S. (2000). *Memorizing: A Phenomenological Study* (2nd ed.). Bloomington, IL: Indiana University Press.

Heidegger, M. (2010). *Being and Time*. Albany, NY: Suny Press.

Merleau-Ponty, M. (2001) *Phenomenology of Perception [Phénoménologie de la perception]*. London: Routledge & Kegan Paul. (First published 1954).

Pallasmaa, J. (2009). Space, Place, Memory and Imagination: The Temporal Dimension of Existential Space. In M. Treib (Ed.), *Spatial Recall: Memory in Architecture and Landscape* (1st ed.). New York: Routledge.

Rossi, A. (1982). *Architettura della città*. Cambridge, MA: MIT Press.

Shusterman, R. (2012). *Thinking through the Body: Essays in Somaesthetics*. New York: Cambridge University.

2 *The Fold*: in search of a new harmony through embodied composition

(Singapore and Germany)

Timothy O'Dwyer

The Fold was a collaborative composing project that was staged in Singapore in 2013, involving musicians from contrasting stylistic and cultural backgrounds. The musicians came together to compose written scores that were subsequently used for improvisation during performances. In this chapter I will be discussing the philosophical background of the initial concepts used to begin the project, which were inspired by Leibniz's *psychic geometry* and Deleuze's ideal of a *New Harmony*, found in his book *The Fold: Leibniz and the Baroque.* Moreover, I develop the idea of the *psychic geometry* in parallel with Mark Johnson's concept of *image schemata* in his book *The Body in the Mind: The Bodily Basis of Meaning, Imagination and Reason* in order to further illustrate how the collaborators interpreted the initial abstract framework and how they embodied these ideas into musical scores and in performance. *The Fold* project explored the process of creating musical works by combining motifs composed by every member of the ensemble. By creating pieces made up of motifs offered by a collective of composer/performers, the project aimed to create a music that represented the individuality of each of the musicians in the group in a more integrated way. Whilst discussing the site-specific nature of the project in Singapore, the 'Deleuzian Baroque' is ever present in the discourse. As conceptual frameworks were embodied by the musicians, their personal stories become intertwined, enabling a 'new harmony' to emerge.

I possess a clear and distinguished zone of expression because I have primitive singularities, ideal virtual events for which I am destined. From this moment deduction unwinds: I have a body because I have a clear and distinguished zone of expression. In fact, that which I express clearly, the moment having come, will concern my body and will act most directly on my body, surroundings, circumstances and environment (Deleuze, 2007, p. 98).

Initially, the musicians gathered in *The Fold* project expressed primitive singularities in the form of their unique cultural and musical experiences. The method of collaboratively composing (in) *The Fold* enabled them to communicate their musical ideas to each other through their bodies and instruments in order to reach thresholds of intensity, conscious and unconscious, ambiental and corporeal, folding forward into the written gesture of the compositional idea, which, in turn, acted directly on their bodies, the sounds that they made, their surroundings and the audience, expressing their clear and unique zones of expression or personality. Through these composed (written) documentations, or virtual (graphic) events, clear zones of expression emerge as their singularities are juxtaposed and compared with one another. The journey of *The Fold* project is a narrative about how distinct individuals with diverse backgrounds came together, worked through a set of shared abstract concepts and created new music collectively.[1]

Practicum: a psychic geometry/image schemata

The individual musicians involved in the Singapore project came from diverse cultural and stylistic backgrounds. Aya Sekine, a Japanese jazz pianist; Vuk Krakovic, a Serbian classical violinist formerly from Cirque du Soleil; Tony Teck Kay Makarome, a Chinese Singaporean jazz bassist who is also steeped in South Indian Carnatic music; Darren Moore, a drummer and electronic musician (also steeped in the Carnatic tradition) born in Scotland and raised in Australia; and myself, an Australian-born saxophonist and composer. This assemblage of musicians reflects the cosmopolitan nature of Singapore, one of the most multicultural city-states in Asia. Having collaborated with all of them in different groups I was well aware of their capabilities as musicians and how they could contribute in distinct ways to the project. I was also aware that they would come to the project with open minds; this was important as they were required, on the one hand, to contribute compositional material that would illustrate their own experiences and, on the other hand, to be able to interpret, improvise and co-create as a collective.

During the process of composing the music in *The Fold*, the musicians were given five preconceived concepts by me to respond to with musical ideas. These 'themes' were directional, points of reference on an imaginary axis, and could be seen as a form of abstract calculus or a *psychic geometry*. The musicians navigated through this landscape, creating motifs guided by points along this allegorical curve of qualities[2] and thresholds, labelled as the Present, Above, Below, Past and Future. These labels or themes created a three-dimensional space of vertical, horizontal and central points, and in themselves were not fixed as objects or even archetypes; they were manoeuvred by the musicians and expressed from each of their inherent perspectives, which might have included the musicians' lived, physical or phenomenal positions in the moment or in the world as well as their experienced or imagined pasts, presents or futures.

To further illustrate how this conceptual framework worked I see a strong correlation between Leibniz' *psychic geometry* and Mark Johnson's concept of *image schemata* in his book *The Body in the Mind: The Bodily Basis of Meaning, Imagination, and Reason*: "...image schemata are not rich, concrete images or mental pictures... They are structures that organize our mental representations at a level more general and abstract than that at which we form mental images" (1987, pp. 23–24). Johnson explains his image schemata as a dynamic system of organising thoughts and ideas; it is not like a template that has fixed parameters and prescriptions. In contrast, the *image schemata* and the *psychic geometry* "are flexible in that they can take on any number of specific instantiations in varying contexts" (Johnson, 1987, pp. 29–30).

Moreover, the *Present, Above, Below, Past and Future* are Deleuzian *events*. They are conglomerates of differential relations, accumulative forces influenced by "tiny perceptions [that] are as much the passage from one perception to another as they are components of each perception" (Deleuze, 2007, p. 87). This axis of qualities and thresholds projects a *psychic geometry* into the landscape of micro-perceptions within the individual musician. It allows them to articulate their previously hallucinatory perceptions[3] into (clear) zones of expression. For Deleuze (2007), "all consciousness is a matter of threshold"; what is interesting is "why the threshold is marked where it is" (p. 89). The thresholds are "affective qualities, confused or even obscured perceptions that resemble something by virtue of Leibniz' projective geometry".[4] They are "natural signs" resembling neither extension nor movement, but are "matter in extension, vibrations, elasticities [...] tendencies of efforts" in motion (Deleuze, 2007, p. 96).

In the context of *The Fold* project, the responses of the musicians to the *psychic geometry/image schemata* of *Present, Above, Below, Past and Future* are musical gestures in the form of melodies, harmony, rhythm or noise. The macro-points of the *Present, Above, Below, Past and Future* framework are not ends in themselves; it is *between* these points of reference and the differential relationships created by them that certain thresholds of consciousness manifest from within each musician. By traversing the 'in between', tiny perceptions are revealed, collected and expressed in written musical forms, reflecting the function of Liebniz's differential calculus, as described by Deleuze:

> *Differential relations always select minute perceptions that play a role in each case*, and bring to light or clarify the conscious perception that comes forth. Thus differential calculus is the psychic mechanism of perception, the automatism that at once and inseparably plunges into obscurity and determines clarity: a selection of minute, obscure perceptions and a perception that moves in clarity.
> (Deleuze, 2007, p. 90)

The musicians navigate and respond to these spheres or thresholds, articulating their perceptions by composing *Cantus Firmi*[5] or fixed melodies. Each note of their Cantus Firmus illustrates little foldings of disquiet, a "spiritualising of dust" (of the compositional process) manifested in perceptions that are not necessarily located in one of these "natural signs" represented by *Present, Above, Below, Past and Future*. They are sounds *prehended* in the passage from one 'natural sign' to another, which only come to be understood as a perception of the macro-point through the relationships constructed along micro-points on the curve of each note's phrase and the *contra punctum* (the musical relationship of one note to another) of the Cantus Firmus. The notes selected by each musician and their inter-relationships within the *contra punctum* are "engaged in differential relations and produce the quality that issues forth at the given threshold of consciousness" (Deleuze, 2007, p. 89).

For example, when a musician decides to compose the note "A", "A" is in a differential relation to the musician and their body – the selection of "A" is in difference to deciding upon any other note: "B", "F" or "D#". "A" is also in differential relation to all other notes in the Cantus Firmus in terms of its harmonic meaning – "A" is differentially related to "B", which is differentially related to "C" and so on.[6] Moreover, the musical notes in the Cantus Firmus become embodied gestures, a collection of points along a curve, tangents that vaguely measure an infinitesimal projection of the clear zone of expression of each musician. In parallel, Wayne Bowman (1998), in *Philosophical Perspectives on Music*, gives this succinct appraisal of Johnson's *image schemata*, which has intersecting points with Leibniz's 'psychic mechanism of perception' and the embodying process:

> Image schemata and metaphorical projections are experiential structures of meaning that are essential to most of our abstract

> understanding and reasoning. And because those structures originate in and remain tied to our bodily experience, the body is always and necessarily in the mind: the body is the eliminable source of human rationality.
>
> (p. 297)

Image schemata – psychic geometry. The musicians interpret these perspectives and graphically represent them in the form of scores; in turn, they perform the scores with their bodies. In the process of doing this, they embody the *image schemata – psychic geometry* through their practice. The resultant sounds are a consequence of their embodiment of the conceptual thresholds and represent Johnson's bodily basis of mind. "Revealing the bodily basis of mind enables us not only to assert, but to show how music is at once a cerebral and a bodily competence" (Bowman, 1998, p. 299).

During this first stage, the musicians were encouraged to respond spontaneously while in isolation to the thresholds of *Present, Above, Below, Past and Future* in composing their Cantus Firmi. This activity happened over a four to five-week period towards the end of 2012 and early 2013. I gave out some brief instructions on what could be interpreted as 'Above' and 'Below', but overall these themes were open for the musicians to interpret. For example, upon reflection, some of the musicians expressed that they composed the motifs based on their own experiences; this made the motifs very personal.

> Each melody reflects on a part of my life, a moment in time or a memory. The most challenging part was having to come up with only one melodic line instead of composing the complete piece of music for the given titles.
>
> (V. Krakovic, personal communication, March 9, 2020)

The challenge of this process for the musicians was to attempt to encapsulate the idea or their emotional and intellectual response within the confines of a simple melody. Some chose to depict distinct aspects of their cultural backgrounds and musical experiences. Figure 2.1 is an example of a Cantus Firmus composed by Krakovic. Originally from Serbia, and now residing in Singapore, the violinist/composer is responding to *The Past* threshold. Composed in the time signature of 9/8 the melody evokes the 'gestural DNA' of his homeland and the music of the Balkans through the rhythmic organization of the phrase (grouped as 12,12,12,123 – 9 beats). I will return to this particular Cantus Firmus later to show how it was integrated and arranged into a larger score.

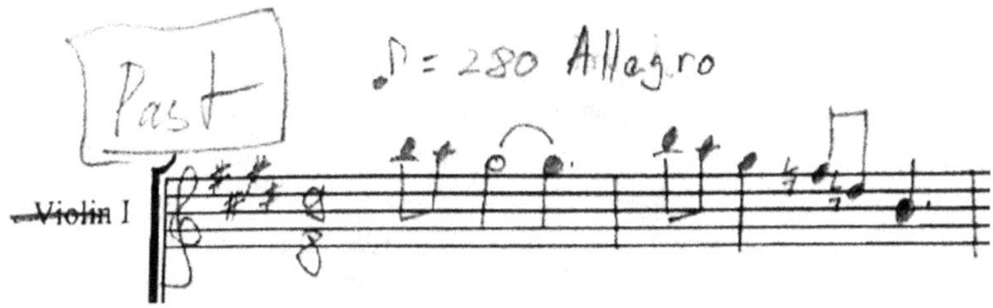

Figure 2.1 Excerpt from *The Past*, V. Krakovic. Courtesy of the artist.

The bass player, Tony Makarome, reflected on the composing process,

> At the time of composing, I was personally struggling with the question of how I can use the influence of my Carnatic music studies (mridangam and vocal) in my compositions (primarily western in approach). This project allowed me to inject these Carnatic elements without bringing attention to them as Carnatic elements.
>
> (T. Makarome, personal communication, March 9, 2020)

As a process whereby composers/performers could trial ideas and concepts, *The Fold* project seemed to enable them to experiment more freely. In contrast to Krakovic, who felt a little confined by the process, Makarome found that because the individual ideas from the different musicians were woven together to make new arrangements, the pressure of coming up with a fully conceived composition was reduced. In view of creating new works involving a collaborative process of compositions, *The Fold* project was a valuable opportunity for participants to take risks. In Figure 2.2, you see the offering of Markarome as a Cantus Firmus that was his response to "*Future*". As someone who was at the beginning of composing with these rhythmic ideas and would develop them into larger works over subsequent years, this gives an embryonic glimpse into the beginnings of a personal style combining Carnatic rhythm concepts in his composed music. Rhythmically, the melody is grouped into a typical Carnatic phrase, as indicated in Figure 2.2 [4+2 | 4+4+2 | 4+4+4]; [4+2 | 4+4+2 | 4+4+4]; [2+2 | 2+2 | 2+2], completing a 21-beat cycle (7 beats per bar × 3 bars). This type of grouping differs from how a usual Western phrase would be rhythmically organised, with an emphasis on phrases 'crossing over' the different beats of the bar. At the same time, Tony has composed the melody

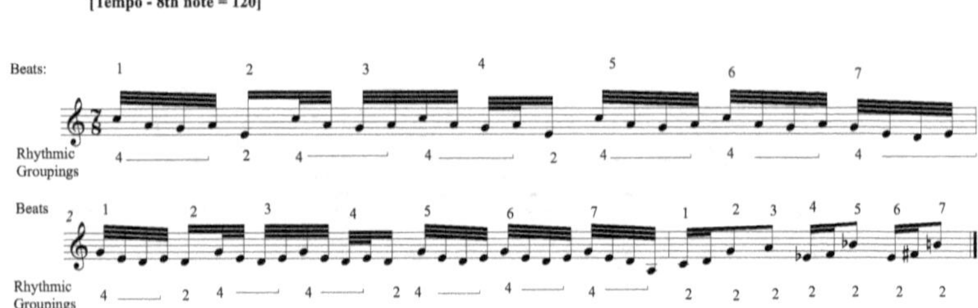

Figure 2.2 "Melody 5, The Future", T. Makarome. Courtesy of the artist.

using a C pentatonic scale, a grouping of notes that has been used to compose music for millennia in China and throughout East Asia. The motif is a combination of Tony's Chinese Singaporean heritage and his deep understanding of the Carnatic tradition. South Indian culture has been prominent in Singapore since the early 19th century. Herein lies a remarkable little microcosm of rich cultures coming together in one motif that could probably only be possible in Singapore and the region, where the cultural heritage of these ethnic groups has lived together for centuries.

Aya Sekine's approach to composing and embodying the abstract geometry was narrative in nature:

> Each of the 5 perspectives had some stories (to me) and I had to draw on my own imagination as well… I usually and always think of 'adding to the story'. At least I try. I like stories, conversations and responses in music making. I bring it 'down' to me, and this wasn't the case for a long time. I used to 'try to create', but around 2012 I had an awakening experience to 'let it come to me' and let me be me.
> (A. Sekine, personal communication, March 9, 2020).

Sekine illustrates through her reflection aspects of body in mind, almost like letting her body guide her through this intuitive approach, 'I bring it "down" to me' further illustrating Deleuze's statement 'I possess a clear and distinguished zone of expression because I have primitive singularities' (2007, p. 98). Through the process, a clear zone of expression emerges whilst interpreting the *psychic geometry – image schemata* as personal narrative. We began this project at the end of 2012, with its first performance at the Esplanade Recital Studio (Singapore) in early 2013. Through *The Fold* project, Sekine's inward transformation of letting the music 'come to me' and 'let me be me' illustrates a valuable mechanism that was in play before the start of *The Fold* project. Moreover, given that the collective activity offered a 'safe space' for her to explore, experiment and take risks, this enabled her to produce more personal responses to the *psychic geometry – image schemata.*

For the drummer Darren Moore, the challenge was actually composing the melody first. As a rhythm player, his natural instinct to composing involved initially thinking about the music from a rhythmical point of view or, as he puts it, "from the bottom up". The process of *The Fold* project engaged him in thinking about the compositional process "from the top down". As an electronic musician, he "also adapted some concepts from using modular synthesizers for example creating rhythmic ideas based on the envelope generator creating a 'bouncing ball' effect where the sound gets quieter as the tempo increases". Creating the effect of sound disappearing into the distance throughout the duration of the gesture. In response to my question about whether his melodies were a reflection of his personality, he responded emphatically: "It's a direct reflection. I don't see how it can be anything otherwise" (D. Moore, personal communication, March 9, 2020). Johnson's *image schemata* reflects this attitude, as explained by Bowman (1998): "The life experiences of the embodied mind are, on Johnson's theory, not separable from its musical ones" (p. 299).

The New Harmony

In Chapter 9 of *The Fold: Leibnitz and the Baroque*, entitled "The New Harmony", Deleuze cleverly plays with the words "concertation" and "concertante". Concertante is a style of composition developed in the late Baroque period, with prominent solo parts for musicians that interact with the ensemble arrangement. The use of the word in this context describes the process of finding accords, that is, forms and harmonic relationships:

> For Leibniz, pre-established harmony has many formulas, each in respect to the spot through which the fold is passing: sometimes it is among principles, mechanisms, or finality, or even continuity and indiscernibles; at others, between the floors [of the Baroque house], between Nature and Grace, between the material universe and the soul, or between each soul and its organic body; and at others again, among substances, simple substances and corporeal or composite substances.
>
> (Deleuze, 2007, pp. 132–133)

During the second phase of arranging, the Cantus Firmi offered by each musician were collected; they were deterritorialized/reterritorialized[7] under the titles of each threshold: for example, the motifs composed by each musician in response to *The Present* theme were arranged into one composition, as were the motifs created in response to *The Above* theme. The musical function of each Cantus Firmus within the arrangement was approached from an infinite perspective and utilized without a priori. Each motif was swiftly juxtaposed with the next – an individual motif could emerge as a bass riff or within a chord sequence; the rhythmic elements of the motif could be isolated into a drum part or as the main melody.[8]

Whilst rehearsing these arrangements in the third stage of the process, the Cantus Firmi were further developed collectively through negotiation and revision – in order to deal with "principles, mechanisms [and] indiscernibles". The pieces were formed into quasi-concertante-*style* works, which meant that they were composed into *tutti* (everyone playing together) as well as solo sections featuring the players in the ensemble as improvising soloists while the rest of the ensemble performed an accompaniment. In Figure 2.3 we see Krakovic's Cantus Firmus integrated into the full score with the other musicians' ideas. In this instance, Krakovic is actually performing (follow the top line in the score and compare it to the handwritten line in Figure 2.1) his own

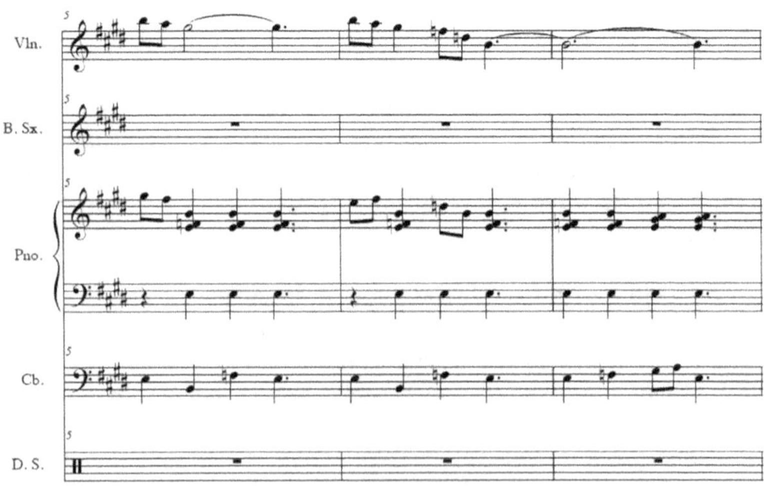

Figure 2.3 Excerpt from the Full Score of "The Past". Illustrating the integration of V. Krakovic, Cantus Firmus.

Cantus Firmus while the other musicians are improvising and playing accompanying figures in response to his original melody. This process of composition was so prevalent in, and intrinsic to, the Baroque era that "many musicologists prefer to speak of the 'concertant' style instead of Baroque music" (Deleuze, 2007, p. 132) when describing the music of the period. This style of composing, especially when the solo parts are improvised, has echoes in jazz music, along with many other folk musics around the world. Analogous to these traditions, the "pieces" are not fixed structures; they are real-time sites of negotiation between the performer-composers in the ensemble.

As a form of music making *The Fold* project harks back to pre-classical ideas in Western music,[9] dissolving the importance and hierarchy of the score or musical work and the composer, and the divisions of labour amongst musicians. In the pre-classical era, performers were composers and improvisers in equal measure. However, the process initiates more than a revision of relationships between musicians performing in an ensemble. The maps or "scores" constructed from the above-mentioned process are Baroque perspectives that create a temporary linear focus and variable relations throughout the structure. Importantly, these maps created in the process of arranging. There are no pre-conceived "forms" (or memory) that the melodies adhere to; the maps resemble written out "comprovisations" (composed improvisations). They are what Deleuze calls "haecceity, becoming, the innocence of becoming" (Deleuze and Guattari, 2004, p. 326).

The arrangements are made up of a flow of disparate melodic ideas that emerged from each of the musician's singular perspectives, unveiling "in a single movement [their] unfathomable depths of tiny and moving folds" (Deleuze, 2007, p. 93). Sekine reflected, "I think the last one which I think is Future, was like a grand celebration of little creatures having a crazy festival" (A. Sekine, personal communication, March 9, 2020). This idea that a community of practice between musicians can be created through collective composition produces a thread back to our past, before 'musical works', to a time of oral traditions which Jacque Attali (2006) describes in his book *Noise: The Political Economy of Music*:

> To my way of thinking, music appears in myth as *an affirmation that society is possible.* That is the essential thing. Its order simulates the social order, and its dissonances express marginalities. *The code of music simulates the accepted rules of society.*
>
> (p. 29)

Ritualistic musical experiences present people with a vital affirmation of the value of sacrificing individuality to produce a continuity. Just as music forges order and unity from chaos, so people come to believe that social association provides protection from the general violence of pre-social existence. "A communal ritual, an activity of the body undertaken and shared by all" (Bowman, 1998, p. 338).

Moreover, the improvisations created by the musicians during performance, in the fourth stage of the project, were not only created as extended or quantified "stuff" – extensions of the written music. They acted on, and became, variations of the "singularities" – between the geometric thresholds of *Present, Above, Below, Past and Future* (Robinson, 2010, p. 194). Through improvisation, the subjective perspective or "point of view" of the musician's position (as co-author – *improve-iser*) within this geometry enabled this "linear focus" to unfold from the materials within the compositions, initiating unique intensities through the *psychic geometry – image schemata* manifested as embodied trajectories in the music. During the performance these singularities were obliterated into intensive linear relationships. The operative function of the score, in a Baroque sense, was a site of transformation and variation within the performance that embodied the collective creativity of the group. The music "lives" in the moment of performance as the musicians are compelled to react to one another's variable intensities. Moreover, what is heard is the intensive quantity, made up of the sum of infinitely small parts. Instead of the score prescribing and defining the curvature, and measuring the rate of change, improvisation enabled the musicians to explore the infinite micro-perceptions and "singularities" between them and the music.

Notes

1 I have used revised excerpts from a previously published work titled 'The Fold: Musical Monads and Baroque Assemblages' in *Symbolism: An Interdisciplinary Journal of Critical Aesthetics 2019*, edited by Natasha Lushetich, generously given permission to be republished by De Gruyter Publishing.

2 Bringing into play the microscopic relationships between the curve and the straight line in Leibniz's geometry. A measuring of points and thresholds is taking place along this metaphorical curve but at a subliminal or psychic level.

3 Deleuze (2007) points out that "*Every perception is hallucinatory because perception has no object.* Our conscious perception has no object" (p. 93) or physical reality. It can only surmise an idea of reality through the differential relations of these micro-perceptions intersecting and folding within the subconscious realms of the individual monad.

4 In comparison to Newton's calculus, Leibniz posited that numbers could actually be infinite, whilst, for Newton, the numbers remained "very small" but nevertheless finite. The results of the theoretical calculus in both cases were the same. However, by allowing there to be a *possibility* of the infinite in his version, Leibniz created the idea of a projective geometry, a vision of geometry as an abstract concept in which the mind could only imagine or project what was potentially limitless; that which could not be defined by finite numbers and was therefore hallucinatory; a geometrical perspective that was subjective and transitory, not objectively represented in mathematical terms alone.
5 *Cantus Firmus* – the first series of notes composed from which all other permutations arise, especially in the composition of fugues and other early forms of Baroque music.
6 Deleuze and Guattari (2004), in *A Thousand Plateaus*, suggest a transformational process during the act of composition and the choices that composers make between writing one note or another, with the notes transcending themselves into "becoming" the composer. For example "Berg's B in *Wozzeck*, Schumann's A" (p. 327).
7 To deterritorialize material in this context is to take it in its original form and recontextualise it to a new location. To reterritorialize material is to change components of the original material and recontextualise it to a new location.
8 This approach to composing is also analogous to Deleuze's "multilinear system" of *becoming*, from *A Thousand Plateaus*: the process

> draws a horizontal, melodic line, the bass line, upon which other melodic lines are superposed; points are assigned that enter into relations of counterpoint between lines… it draws a vertical, harmonic line or plane, which moves along the horizontals but is no longer dependent upon them; it runs from high to low and defines a chord capable of linking up with the following chords.
>
> (Deleuze and Guattari, 2004, p. 325)

9 Musicians in the Baroque period and before were improvisers and composers in equal measure. A time before the 'score' became a dominant concept, and hierarchies of composer/conductor/performer were established. As Lydia Goehr suggests in *The Imaginary Museum of Musical Works*, it "came into being in the late eighteenth century, giving an 'institutionalised centrality' to music making, and contributed to the important historical idea of the 'musical work'" (1992, p. 96).

References

Attali, J. (2006) *Noise: The Political Economy of Music*. (B. Massumi. Trans). Minneapolis, MN: University of Minnesota Press.

Bowman, W.D. (1998) *Philosophical Perspectives on Music*. New York: Oxford University Press.

Deleuze, G. (2007) *The Fold: Leibniz and the Baroque*. Minneapolis, MN: Regents of the University of Minnesota.

Deleuze, G. and Guattari, F. (2004) *A Thousand Plateaus.* (B. Massumi. Trans). London: Continuum (Original work published 1980).

Goehr, L. (1992) *The Imaginary Museum of Musical Works: An Essay in the Philosophy of Music*. Oxford: Oxford University Press.

Johnson, M. (1987) *The Body in the Mind: The Bodily Basis of Meaning, Imagination and Reason*. Chicago, IL: University of Chicago Press.

Robinson, K. (2010) 'Towards a Political Ontology', in *Deleuze and the Fold: A Critical Reader*, ed. Sjoerd van Tuinen and Niamh McDonnell. Basingstoke, Hampshire: Palgrave Macmillan.

3 Human Origami: uncovering meta-levels of corporeal embodiment through movement improvisation

(Singapore, UK, Ireland, Germany, USA)

Susan Sentler and Glenna Batson

Introduction

Corporeality locates itself within contemporary cultural studies, primarily within discourses on embodiment. Many of these discourses matured between the 1970s and 1990s (Bresler, 2004). Dance scholar Susan Foster defined the study of corporeality in the 1990s as one that "seeks to vivify the study of bodies through a consideration of bodily reality, not as natural or absolute given but as a tangible and substantial category of cultural experience" (Foster, 1996, p. xi). The word 'corporeality' has traditionally referred to the states and qualities of the physical or material body. Today, however, the plural, 'corporealities', is more commonly used to suggest a body that is multiple, volatile and extended. As Michel Bernard (philosopher of aesthetics of dance, choreography and theatre) states, "[d]espite or beyond differences in approach, contemporary philosophers and aesthetic theorists agree to radically subvert the traditional category of 'body' and purpose an original plural, dynamic and random vision…[one] of plastic and spectral connotations…" (Bernard, 2001, p. 21).

The current resurgence of the subject of corporeality within dance (Cooper-Albright, 2013) suggests a need to look deeper into the shared nature and meaning of human movement, and that of dance within contemporary society. The body-when-dancing is more than an anatomical body – an identity that cannot be defined statically. Dance holds within it the infinite potential of transmitting not *one* bodily identity but many bodies, affects and meanings. In essence, dance is the practice of 'corporeal difference' (Chatterjee, 2017, p. 283).

The aim of this chapter is to describe key elements of an improvisational movement process called Human Origami (HO). The authors created this process as an exploratory movement practice designed to generate multiple corporealities. HO, then, can be viewed as a process of generating a corporeality of becoming.

Multi-media and dance artist Susan Sentler, and dance educator Glenna Batson began to research the possibilities of this creative practice in 2013, research that is ongoing. The initial intent was to explore new pathways for contemporary dancers and students to go beyond the boundaries of traditional training in movement creation using this improvisational approach. The collaboration took place both in situ and virtually in creating different events, workshops and platforms in, among others, London; Coventry; Berlin; Limerick; Durham, NC, USA; and Singapore. In this chapter, they relate the origin and hallmark processes of this somatically based approach to embodied practice research. They touch upon its relationship to other discourses that bridge the biological and the aesthetic. Descriptive of an aesthetic relationship is *signs of a nest*, Sentler's dance and multi-media installation on the corporeal juxtaposition of absence/presence of the performing body, as described later in this chapter.

Somatic identities

Human bodies, through their sheer (and shared) physicality, articulate meaning – whether incidental or intended. At the same time, such corporeality is "slippery" (Cooper-Albright, 2013, p. 57) – an emerging and emergent phenomenon (Manning, 2009, p. 13) – and therefore, a "body at work is *a sensing body in movement*" (Manning, 2007, p. xiii). Bridging between scientific and artistic meanings, dance scholar Ann Cooper-Albright defines corporeality as "an intertwining of sensation and perception where the body remains anchored as the central scope of awareness" (Cooper-Albright, 2017, p. 58). Then Cooper-Albright adds a degree of specificity within the creative act of artistic dance making, where one needs "to learn to appreciate the elusive contours of somatic meaning" (ibid., p. 58). These 'elusive contours' emerge from what is 'inscribed' on our bodies – the imprint – historical, sociocultural, political and environmental. What we bear is a 'somatic'[1] body, that is, an inscription on, within and through the moving, living body. These imprints manifest as movement dynamics that can be read as affects, gestural styles and emotional tone (Sheets-Johnstone, 2012). Other imprints go unrecognised. These are more subtle and whispered, hidden within first-person experience, covert and not readily apparent or shared. Regardless, they enter into and influence our pathways of choice-making.

In their creation and development of HO, the authors introduced this work to Singapore. This begged the question: does a specific type of corporeality arise within their work that could be identified as 'Asian'?

As previously noted – but now with deeper implications for ethnicity – dance shares the ontological slippery-ness of identity. It explores movement in ways that afford dancers an experience of 'a plane of open and divergent becomings' (Colebrook, 2005, p. 5). One focus for choreographers is, for example, to subject dancers to an experiential playing field of 'moving identities'. Thus 'identity' is not fixed but fluid, 'changing many times, not only within each dance, but also over the course of each dance (and within each dancer's career)' (Roche, 2015, p. 150). In becoming the agent of changing corporeality within artistic dance-making, the dancer readily meets this flux of context and material, exploring each moment of the unfolding dance as an 'autopoeietic emergence' (ibid., p. 161). Further, such corporealities are empathically shared with other dancers and the audience. Many factors influence how a dance is taken on and interpreted through the dancers' movements as well as how it is perceived by an audience. This phenomenon occurs, even if the same dance is being performed or witnessed. This shared kin-aesthetic and empathic state, moving and being moved, come together as an aesthetic corporeal experience (Smith and Roche, 2015). Thus, it bears repeating that dance is the practice (the performative expression) of a multiplicity of corporeal differences.

At the same time, one common denominator shared by human beings is their capacity for bodily folding and unfolding. This movement dynamic of condensing and expanding is buried deeply within our biopsychic archive. Folding is the basic movement repertoire among human beings. From our earliest gestation, the embryonic folding-unfolding continuum creates a body without a functioning brain or nervous system in less a month (Batson, 2017). The processes within HO, then, can be viewed (experienced) as a means of revisiting one's historicity (see Batson, 2017 for description of this approach to the somatic practice of HO). Herein lies an opportunity to become conscious of all that is beneath the superficial body surface, qualities buried *within* the bodily tissues that embody the history of development and harbour the meaning of life experience. Even at this micro-level of human development, the bodily 'imprint' is *epigenetic*, the sum total of multiple factors that bear on the embryo (O'Neill, 2015). This suggests that even at the earliest stage, a corporeal 'imprint' is arguably cultural as well as biological (ref). Since the processes of HO are aimed at engaging the entire somatic imprint, it may well be that the dancer comes in contact with ephemeral (pre-gravity) memories that formed within the embryo's fluid environment (Williamson, 2010).

Human Origami – perceiving multiplicity

For centuries, paper origami has been a centrepiece of ceremonial ritual and educational play. HO at once partakes of this tradition but largely from its creative impulse, rather than its geometric operations. The human body cannot fold as paper does. It cannot collapse, crush or crease in the same manner. Yet HO and paper origami share the fluidity of perception of human potential and, therefore, the aesthetic of potentially infinite capabilities.

To better understand the sense of tactile corporeality within the material reality of folding requires a shift away from habitual visual perception. When perception becomes palpable (felt), a simple fold reveals a depth of dimensional vectors, directions and dynamics. The fold can be conceived of as a moving potential, a trajectory without a perceptual end. One sees and senses the dynamics embedded in the points of closure and small interstices in a single fold in a piece of paper (Figure 3.1).

One experiences movement – its line, direction, depth, softness; an array, a current of moving qualities that transforms the habitual and commonplace into a mutable perceptual landscape. Take a moment to gaze at a common bed sheet or clothing, loosely draped over a chair (Figure 3.2).

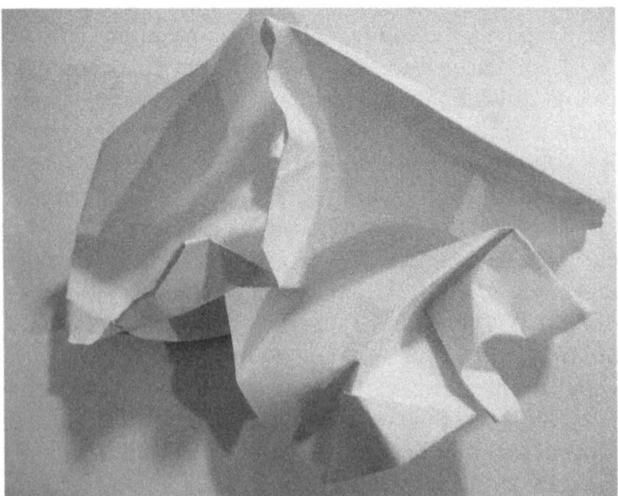

Figure 3.1 Folded paper. Photographer: Susan Sentler.

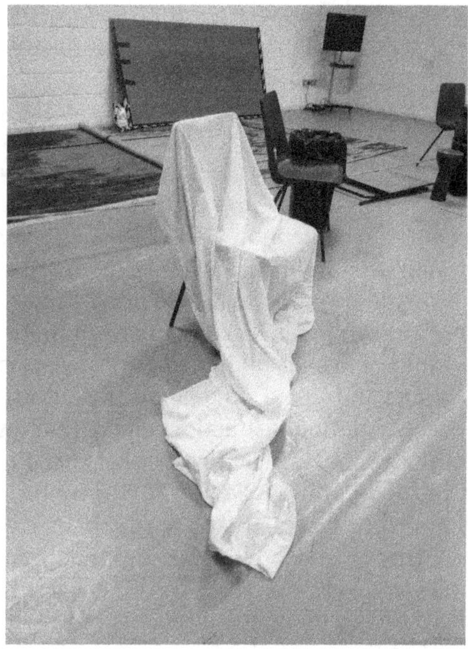

Figure 3.2 Fabric, during HO workshop, London, January 2015. Photographer: Susan Sentler.

Within moments, the viewer goes from seeing the material 'it' to sensing a multiplicity of changing affects. A mere bed sheet becomes a 'corpus' as one's perception-cum-bodily sensations deepen into the folds (foldings) of the material.

In HO, folding allows for the exploration of the dimensions of inner depth (covert enfolding) as well as the dimensions of outward expression (overt unfolding). When improvising with folding, the body takes on a multiplicity of gestural 'corporealities', biomechanical, phenomenological and aesthetic. Therein lies a perceptual paradox where two become one – where two (sides) of matter *incorporate* something of the outside world, invaginating into the surround and adjoining surfaces to become one. As the body folds, any crease in the body can be perceived as having the quality of duality of touch – a feeling of touching and simultaneously being touched. Herein lies an embodied logic that provided insight into an ontology of becoming, a specific corporeality wherein the end is not specified – what 'becomes' is not a finished product but rather an open-ended, infinite continuum of embodiment, which is extended and conflictual.

To explicate this idea further than the multiplicity in bodily becoming, HO transfigures the known identity – one-and-only material corpus – into a moving continuum of change, thereby becoming a 'somatic' body or, simply, 'soma'.[2] The soma acquires a materiality that goes beyond the ease of labelling. While the corpus might be limited materially (anatomical matter), the moving body transmits the capacity for infinite perception – real and palpable. When folding inwards (enfolding) or unfolding outwards (expanding), the moving consciousness extends towards fluid involutions and evolutions that have no fixed beginning or end. The folding body becomes something like cloth, a 'tessuto', the skin taking on the capacity of endless textures, weaves, grains and layers. The paradox is at once a process of individuation (differentiation/distinction) and of shape-shifting transparency. In becoming more transparent, the somatic body yields a visibility of sophisticated pathways. An ability to continuously fall into surprise and yet anchor buoys along the voyages to 'hold on' to the sensations – and, thereby, the bodily shapings that occur in time.

Roland Barthes evolved a textural theory suggesting that 'tissue' plays a generative role in an ongoing process of art-making – a continuous 'interweaving' that renders clear attributions of agency difficult (Barthes, 1981). In the case of dance – and, in this case, of HO in particular – the interweaving of body and environment become inseparable as an extended corporeality. These relations between movements and processes are interwoven, dynamic and multi-layered; deeply rooted in the physical body; and potentially transcendent.

Human Origami – a snapshot

In 2013, Batson conceived of Human Origami when she was an honorary fellow at Trinity Laban Conservatoire of Music and Dance London, UK. She desired to create a unique somatically based, improvisational movement practice, that is, a novel process that did not derive from any previous movement training. At the same time, such practice-based research should foster corporeal emergence, a fluid state of ontological becoming that was free of pre-conceived goals and outcomes. Here, she met Susan Sentler, then dance faculty senior lecturer, and the collaboration began.

Batson was initially inspired by the writings on folding of French phenomenologist Gilles Deleuze in his book *The Fold: Leibniz and the Baroque* (Deleuze, 1993). Deleuze departed from mainstream philosophy, creating instead a conceptual meta-aesthetic of the fold as a continuum, one that underscores the interwoven materiality of self, society and the soul. The treatise is, in one sense, a Möbius strip wherein folding and unfolding express inexhaustible multiplicity and difference. The fold is the continuous and infinite dimension of depth. To paraphrase Deleuze, the smallest unit of matter is not the point but the fold… (ibid.). This phrase, for Batson, provided a springboard for the process-based practice in folding.

While Deleuze did not explicitly explicate a theory of the body, nor invent an approach to movement practice, his references to the corporeal are copious, though indirect (Hughes, 2017). For Deleuze, the body transcends matter through its agency (ibid.), the quality of humans to act autonomously, empowered by their potential to create. Agency, then, is 'a site for creative conceptual-corporeal experimentation' (ibid., p. 5). As the pedagogical scaffold for HO took shape, the practice provided both a space and a place for practicing agency through movement improvisation. Exploring folding patterns provided a multidimensional depth of relations that arose within kinaesthetic consciousness (see Batson 2017, for a description of the fundamental elements and processes, and Appendix 1, for an extract from a practice script) (Figures 3.3–3.7).

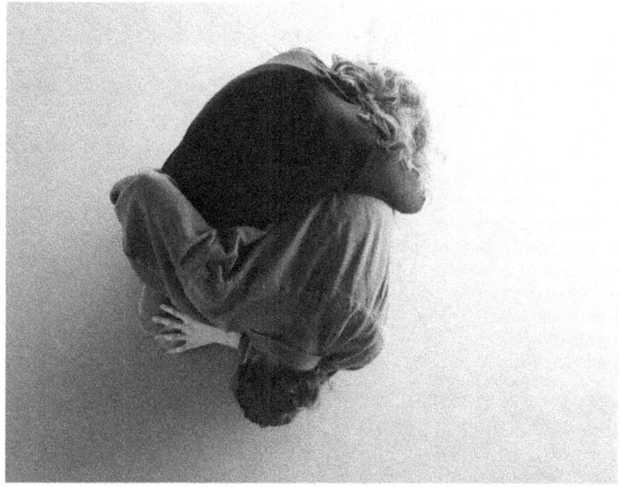

Figure 3.3 Images from various workshops in UK and Singapore since 2013 start of HO research. Photographer: Susan Sentler.

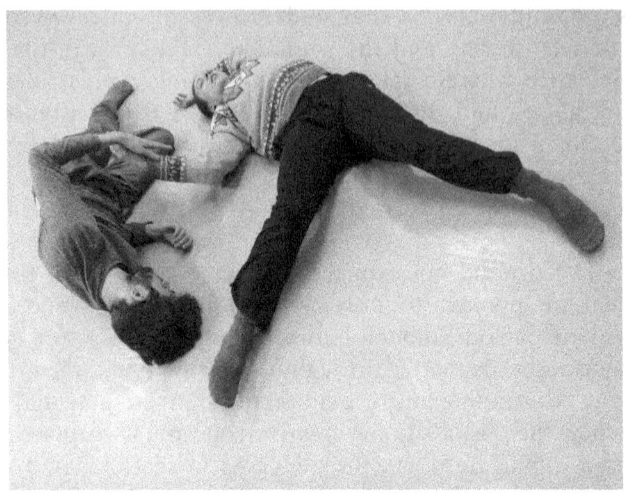

Figure 3.4 Images from various workshops in UK and Singapore since 2013 start of HO research. Photographer: Susan Sentler.

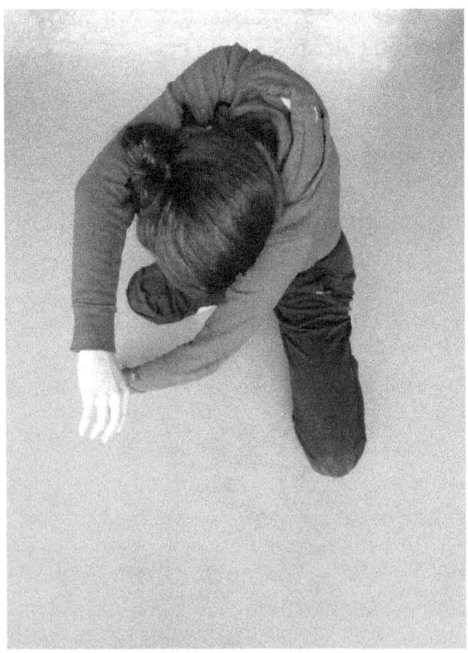

Figure 3.5 Images from various workshops in UK and Singapore since 2013 start of HO research. Photographer: Susan Sentler.

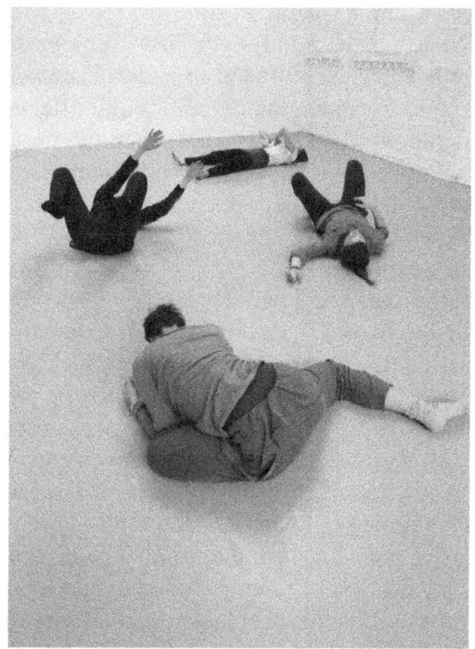

Figure 3.6 Images from various workshops in UK and Singapore since 2013 start of HO research. Photographer: Susan Sentler.

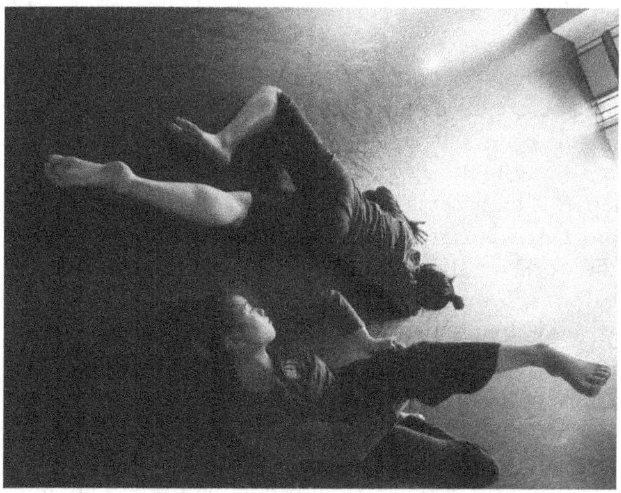

Figure 3.7 Images from various workshops in UK and Singapore since 2013 start of HO research. Photographer: Susan Sentler.

Over the course of their collaboration, the authors evolved a working somatic pedagogy, emphasising sensory awareness to body-in-space, while the dancers improvised. They honed a unique language – one that was mutually enriched by the visual, tactile and kinaesthetic imagery prompts, and the changing dynamics and affects of the improvising dancers. Just how the images unfold in the iterative process is not of the mind alone. New movements (and identities) emerge from the collision and collusion of epi-phenomenal elements. The process speaks of bodily emergence-y, the movement of the bodymind nested in a spatially fluid landscape.

This open method offered a path for exploring corporeal creativity – a nested landscape of internal and external elements that are generative, inspirational, evocative and provocative. While originally designed to enhance dancers' perceptual skills, the process went beyond skill learning. The folding explorations gave way to a multiplicity of movement patterns – a fractal field of movement potential which tapped into unknown sources of creativity. Improvisational structures gave rise to an embodied ontology of becoming whose unfixed boundaries were iterative, non-linear and liminal. The teachers relied heavily on an iterative process of re-entry, one in which dancers could go back into the 'corpus' of a fold that had already been explored through new entry points within the body. Re-entering a fold within the context of a movement theme lends itself to distillation of movement expression – nudging the dance-maker (choreographic mover) to find the essence, the art, of what she wishes to communicate physically. It bears mentioning that this creative 're-entry' allows for sophisticated bodily shaping, a fractal nugget in which the mover can continually unearth novel movement facets. Thus, the distillation does not 'erase' what came before but holds it within the historicity of the bodily exploration, alive and fluid.

It is in their somatic approach to improvisation of HO that the authors depart – by necessity – from Deleuze's logical scaffold. In *One Manifesto Less*, Deleuze writes of a 'process of abstraction'. He critiques the works of Italian director Carmelo Bene, conceiving of his theatrical work as evolving through a process of continuous variation, one that is initiated and sustained by subtraction. HO does not work by subtracting or pruning unneeded elements of performance to release new potentialities which are 'present' and 'actual' (Chiesa, 2012). In Human Origami, nothing is lost. The iterative process of re-entry *through movement* re-incorporates all lived explorations back into a process that frees movement from becoming fixed, a holding pattern on which to hang identity. There is a letting go of ownership of gesture and a recycling of movement elements back into the fluid matrix of the moving body. Nothing 'disappears' or is 'amputated', so to speak. The material dissolves into the batter of moving matter and is reconfigured. The process is designed to liberate the dancer from interferences that inhibit perceptual openness and agility. Iterative re-entry fosters a self-regulating form of problem-generating and -solving through corporeal reabsorption and reconfiguring. What *is* eliminated are interfering patterns of tension and habits that restrict potential creativity, which continually vibrates with new possibilities.

signs of a nest – from somatics to art

After collaborating extensively with Batson on HO, Sentler began to use it in her own pedagogy as well as explore and exhibit it within her creative practice in a number of multi-media art forms. A specific example is *signs of a nest* (2017), a dance and multi-media installation work orchestrating moving and still image, sound, object and the absence/presence of the performing body. The installation took place at the Institute of Contemporary Arts Singapore (ICAS) Brother Joseph McNally Gallery in association with LASALLE College of the Arts. It was a confluence of artistic elements – corporeal, environmental and technological – one that exposed both performers and audience to novelty in an Asian setting. It was rooted in the activity which Sentler coined as 'nesting'. Throughout this time the performers engage in a ritual reaction to intimate detailed photographic images that arise from the Singaporean HDBs (Housing Development Board, public housing). The dancers respond with a continuous folding of their bodies, navigating through non-fixed, improvisational pathways, arriving in 'subversive, hidden nested states'. In this iteration Sentler worked with three dancers, each performing in a solo capacity, the three alternating in a durational rotor. This specific site housed intricate architectural details that afforded multiple variations for the activities of folding arriving to nested states. The performance element of the installation begins with each dancer taking off their sandals as one does when entering many Singaporean homes. The dancer then takes the iPad, which screens 150 images, looping every five seconds (Figures 3.8–3.12).

She engages in a robotic-like viewing of the intimate domestic images as she meanders through the space. At a certain point the soloist becomes stimulated by an image; this, in turn, shifts her into a simple

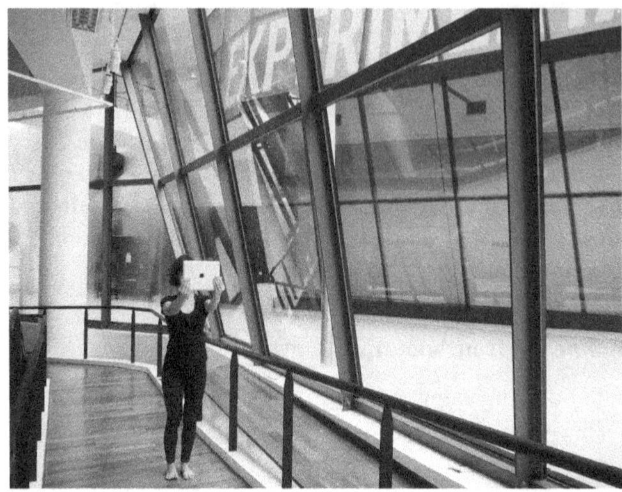

Figure 3.8 Image of performer, in ritual, with iPad in space. Photographer: Susan Sentler.

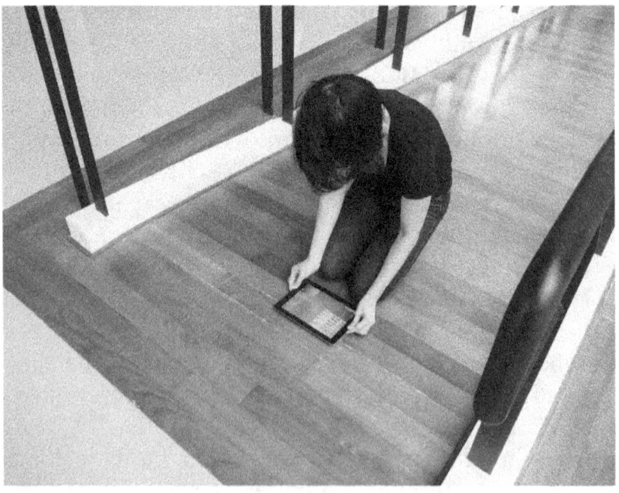

Figure 3.9 Image of performer, in ritual, kneeling before moving into nesting state. Photographer: Susan Sentler.

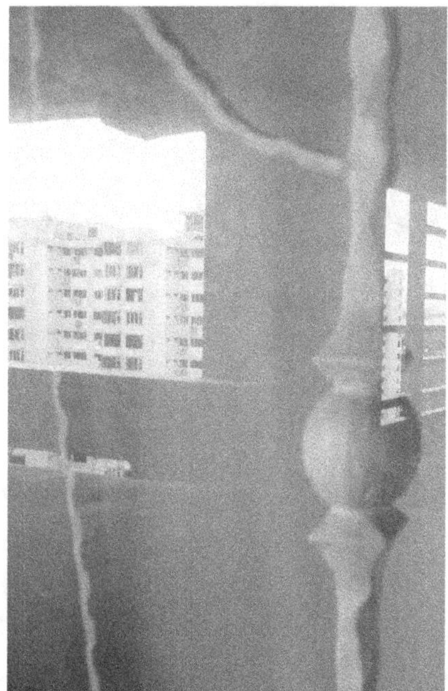

Figure 3.10 Three images within *signs of a nest* film used in installation. Photographer: Susan Sentler.

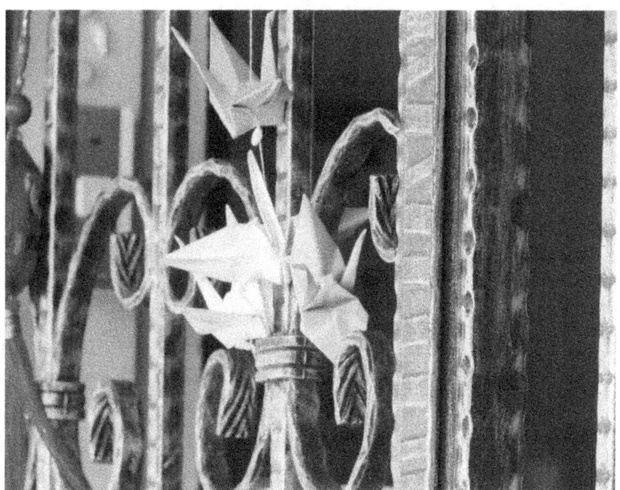

Figure 3.11 Three images within *signs of a nest* film used in installation. Photographer: Susan Sentler.

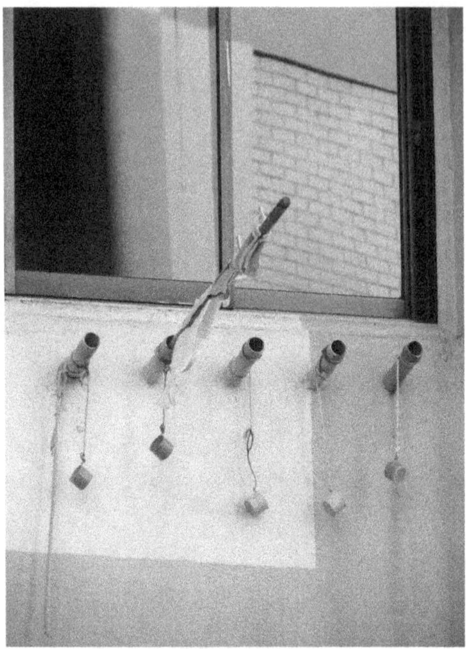

Figure 3.12 Three images within *signs of a nest* film used in installation. Photographer: Susan Sentler.

ritual, kneeling to settle and place the iPad on the ground. Her body begins the nesting engagement, continuous exploration of the folding action. The spatial landscape of the gallery embodies slopes, openings, closures, crevasses, levels and stairs, all stimulating intriguing bodily responses: the folds from within voyaging out, the outer folds drifting in. Also, it is worth nothing that the gallery space is enclosed by a membrane of glass, allowing for multiple perspectives of visibility for the viewer. The body folds and unfolds in a rhythmic play of dynamics, speed and space (from inside and outside) until it surrenders into a subversive hidden nested state. Here, the state is held in vibrational stillness for about one minute, after which the dancer recovers to begin again. The nest not only exists in the space but also in the

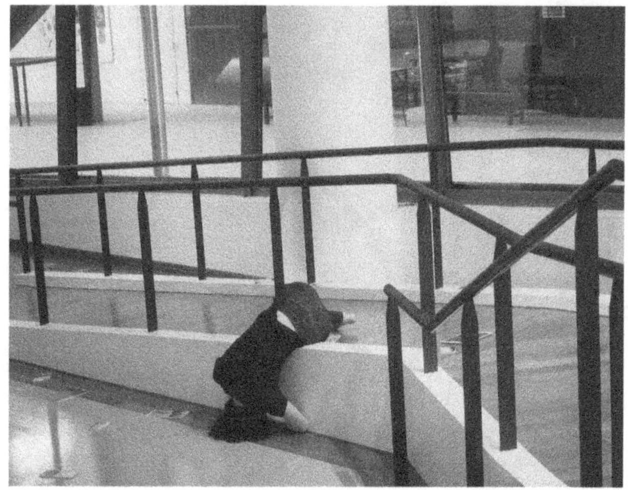

Figure 3.13 Examples of different configurations of nesting states in play with landscape of gallery site. Photographer: Susan Sentler.

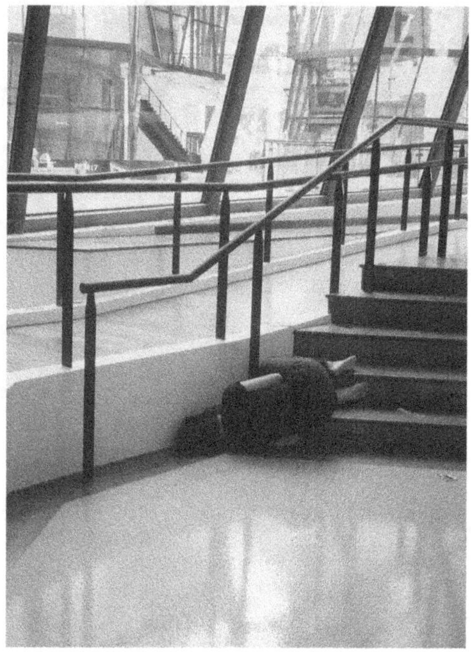

Figure 3.14 Examples of different configurations of nesting states in play with landscape of gallery site. Photographer: Susan Sentler.

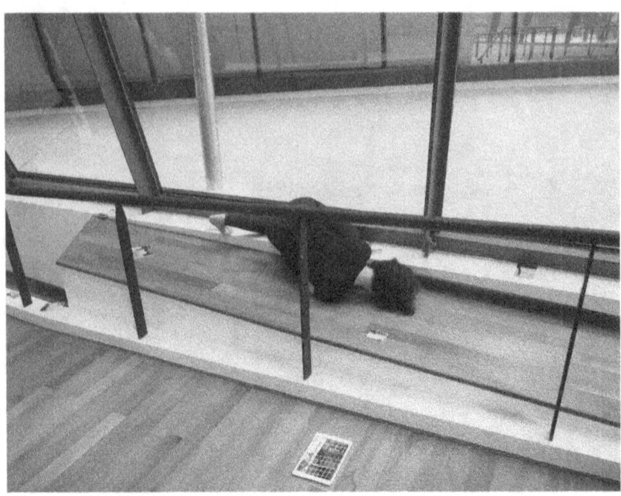

Figure 3.15 Examples of different configurations of nesting states in play with landscape of gallery site. Photographer: Susan Sentler.

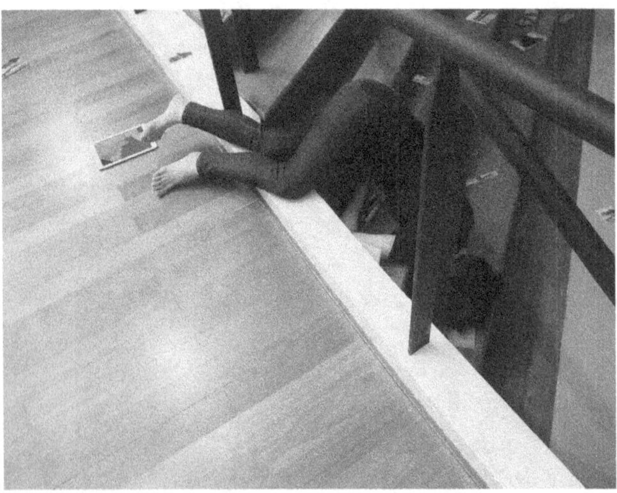

Figure 3.16 Examples of different configurations of nesting states in play with landscape of gallery site. Photographer: Susan Sentler.

multiple ways in which the dancer becomes nested within the space (Figures 3.13–3.16).

Throughout *signs of a nest*, Sentler develops a manner in which the play of folds exists not only in the performer's body but also within the images themselves and through the curation of the objects in the gallery space. By consciously working with this concept, iterative re-entry appears in the manner in which all elements of the work dissolve into a material fluidity, re-associating and layering one into the other. Sentler further creates an improvisational scaffold in which she explores multiple avenues of body yielding – the opening and closing of the performer's body, circling and wayfaring through the space. The space and all the elements of becoming can be read as one body as well as multiple bodies. While the somatic body is given an improvisational structure, one shaped by a sophisticated choreographic voice, the possibilities for folding movement patterns is endless – the body becoming material, the material becoming body, yielding agency to each individual performer within the scope of the score and ultimately agency to the viewers in the manner in which they associate and engage with the folding mass (Figures 3.17–3.19).

The interplay between dancer and environment destabilizes the usual state of a nest as a cosy, comfortable and safe place to land. Rather, hidden subversive states emerge – transitory configurations of human animal and home, a transformative morphing hybrid of body, material and place. The impression was that this form belonged

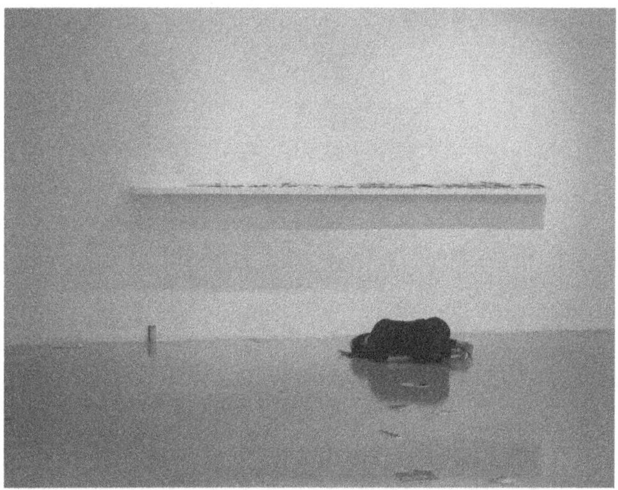

Figure 3.17 Examples of nesting states in the open gallery space. Photographer: Susan Sentler.

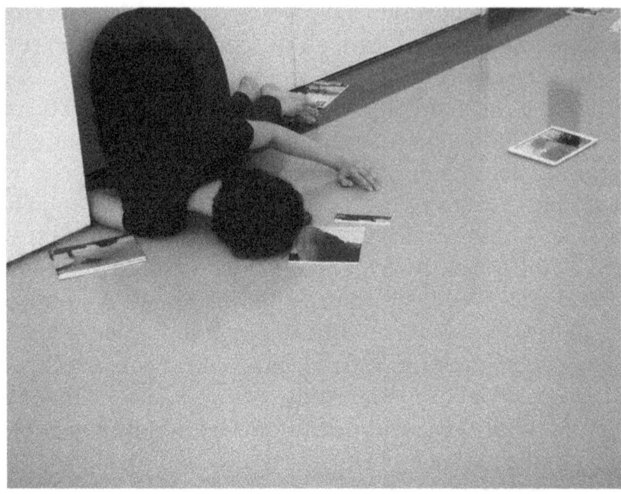

Figure 3.18 Examples of nesting states in the open gallery space. Photographer: Susan Sentler.

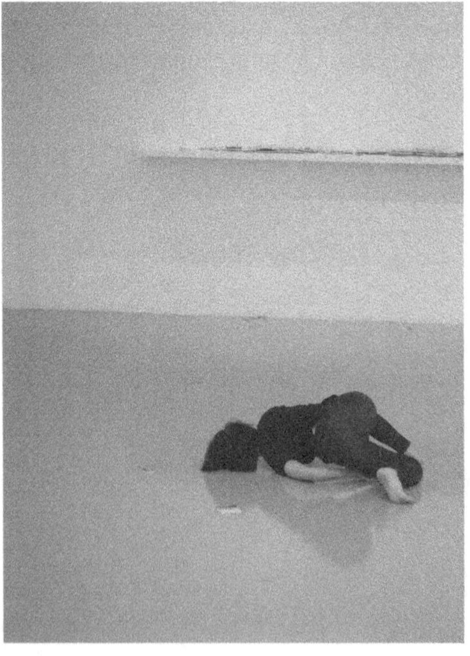

Figure 3.19 Examples of nesting states in the open gallery space. Photographer: Susan Sentler.

everywhere and nowhere, a sense of belonging that blurred the body from the embedded landscape.

The process is liquid, slipping through one's grasp and one's conceptions of what to do, and what to do next. The result is the exact antithesis of a formed sculptured body. The structured improvisational landscape of objects, sounds, and images is constantly reconfiguring through movement and the variability of time and space. Allowing for a multiplicity of changing corporeality in this liquid form is sophisticated in the sense of agency, one free of personal control that pre-determines movement goals and imposes itself on movement freedom. The body is here both an existential prosthesis and an environment. These states are not static, snug or soothing. They are a fleeting form of belonging everywhere and nowhere, a form that is abstracted, blurred and hazy, yet clearly recognizable as a state, a nest.

The "hidden" part of this state also implies gendered context and female embodiment. In contrast to this state of hiddenness, the photographic markers that the dancers used to highlight and mark the spot they had visited, that in which they had nested, and which accumulated over time, were of the deconstructed bodily fragments of a male figure resting in an HDB [a Singaporean housing estate]. The body of the male figure was open, splayed, showed no sense of vulnerability. (Figures 3.20–3.22).

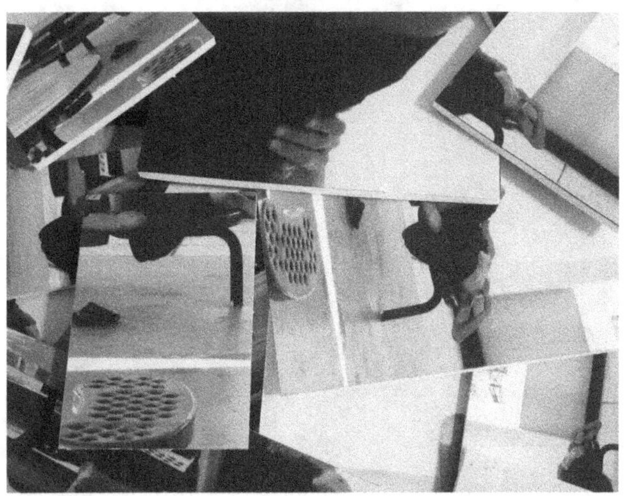

Figure 3.20 Example of *markers*, multiple deconstructed images, of photography of male figure nesting. Photographer: Susan Sentler.

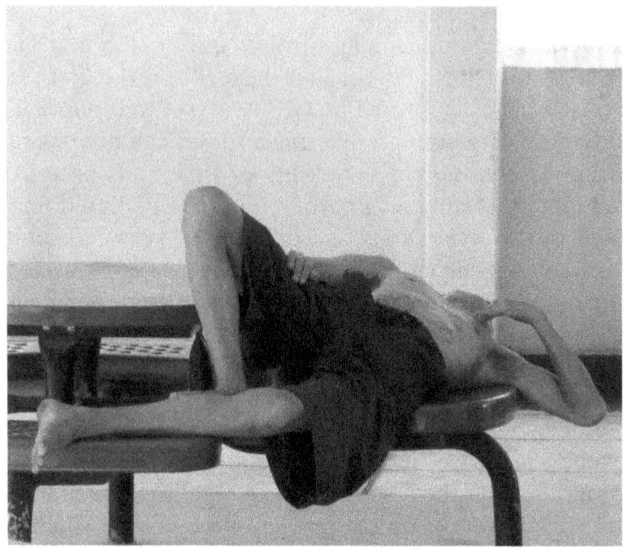

Figure 3.21 Example of markers, multiple deconstructed images, of photography of male figure nesting. Photographer: Susan Sentler.

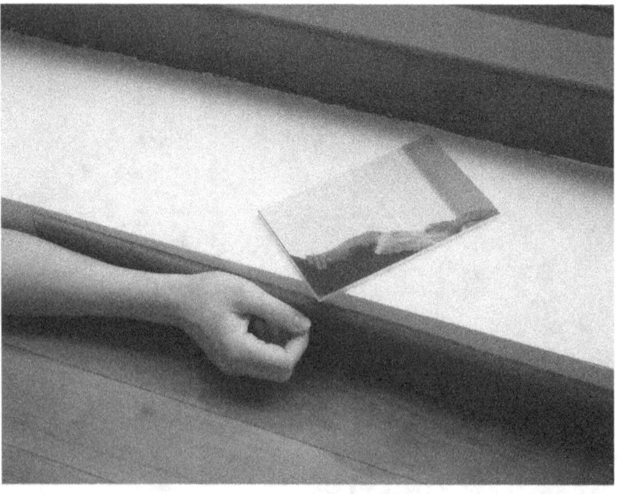

Figure 3.22 Example of markers, multiple deconstructed images, of photography of male figure nesting. Photographer: Susan Sentler.

The subversive element is located in the concealed working of the nest, which is a simultaneous folding inwards and outwards that includes belonging, accumulating and sedimentation of posture, movement and affect but also departure and abandonment. In each nest, there is a germ of abandonment, of moving on, of oblivion and obliteration. The folding activity became a way to discover, encourage and proliferate new pathways and new resting arrivals (Sentler, 2019).

These – everywhere and nowhere – appearing and disappearing forms that yield a clear sense of home and belonging, and yet simultaneously are subversive, subtly agitating and disruptive as well as abstracted, blurred and hazy, are found within the full environment of the installation. The concept of the fold provides a duality of interpretation, of a stark corporeality against the hidden workings of the nest: how the sediment of posture exhibits corporeal extremes of restraint (internal wrapping) as well as lack of restraint (abandonment, oblivion and obliteration). Furthermore the work yields an expansion of the sense of corporeality, a multiplicity of corporealities – of body, of state, of the multi-media installation landscape – all emerging through an artistic rendering of folding (Figures 3.23–3.28).

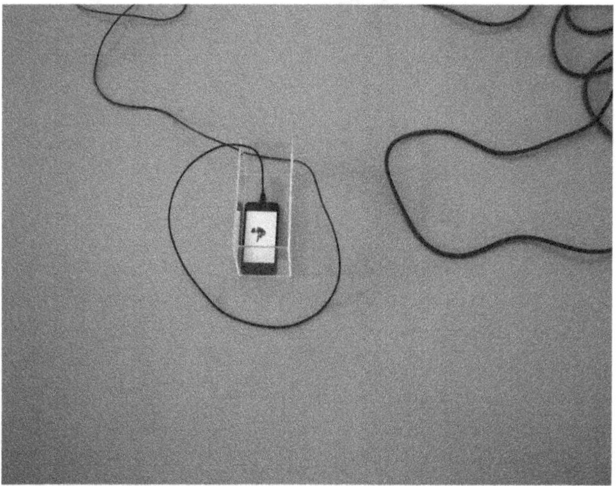

Figure 3.23 Images of other installation elements within *signs of a nest*. Photographer: Susan Sentler.

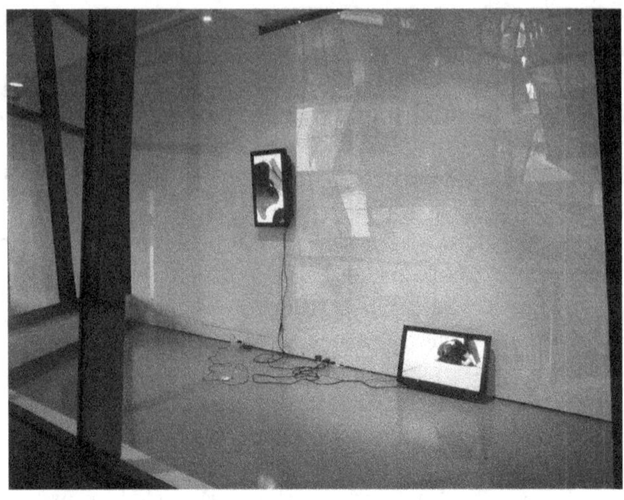

Figure 3.24 Images of other installation elements within *signs of a nest*. Photographer: Susan Sentler.

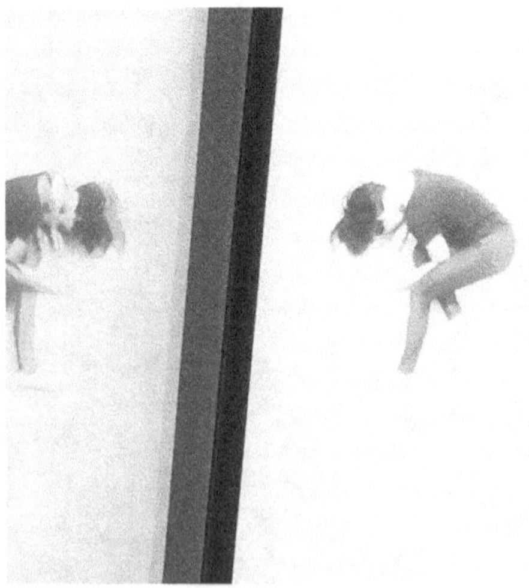

Figure 3.25 Images of other installation elements within *signs of a nest*. Photographer: Susan Sentler.

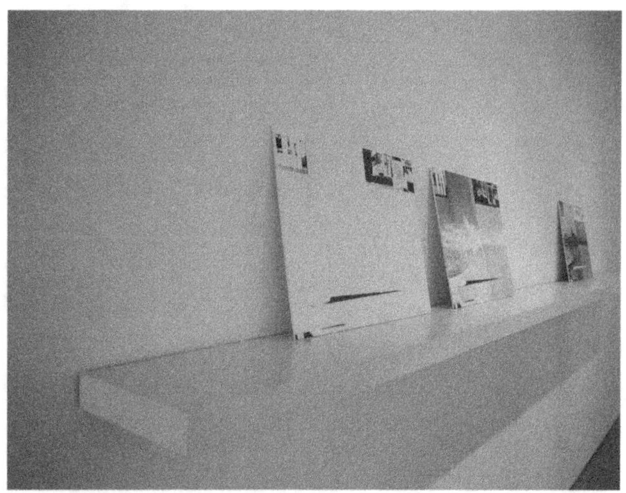

Figure 3.26 Images of other installation elements within *signs of a nest.* Photographer: Susan Sentler.

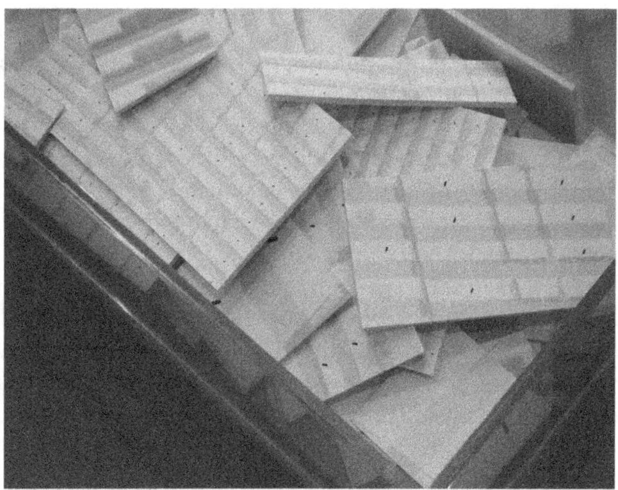

Figure 3.27 Images of other installation elements within *signs of a nest.* Photographer: Susan Sentler.

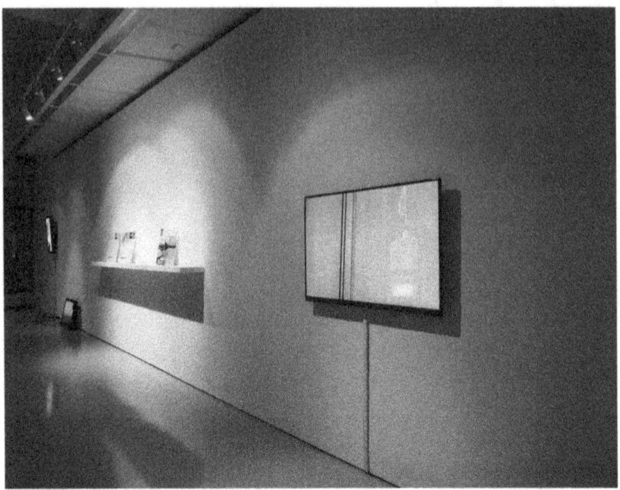

Figure 3.28 Images of other installation elements within *signs of a nest*. Photographer: Susan Sentler.

Closing summary

Human Origami is a process of folding that, at once, captures a fundamental part of the human movement repertoire while offering an exploration of multiple corporealities.

As a movement-centred improvisation, HO offers many inroads into corporeal multiplicity, holding within its processes the mystery of our infinite consciousness. Transcendent yet grounded in the most pedestrian of acts it puts reader and participant alike in touch with the body's most intimate and infinite worlds.

The authors have shown here how this improvisational movement process can at once be a form of investigation into corporeal ontology and an impetus for art-making. The beauty of creatively working from the concept of the fold allows for not only a constant sensation of transformation but permitting the arrival of imagery whose aesthetic must yield to open-ended readings and meanings of corporeality.

Acknowledgement

We would like to thank all the collaborators, dancers and participants thus far within the scope of our research. Most notably those dancers who began the journey with us: Clémentine Télesfort, Stefania Pinato,

Christopher Spraggs and Belinda Papavasiliou. And the dancers who contributed to the making and/or performing of *signs of a nest*: Stella Papi, Valerie Lim, Chan Sze-Wei and Yarra Ileto.

Appendix

Example of Folding script, originally used on January 24, 2015, with students from Trinity Laban Conservatoire of Music and Dance, held at Laurie Grove Studios, London.

Session 5

Looking at the sheet draped over the chair Lying on the back Noticing the landscape underneath, folding and reverse folding of the landscape of your own being meeting the floor, the positive space of the contact, the negative space and the continuity of what is behind – what touches and what sequences from the touch to its reverse. […] we have breath inside of us as a constant, a rhythm, a tone…being aware of how those tones are changing so that any one small crevice, any one small fold from the back of the neck to the back of the head, the forearm into the wrist, the inner thigh to the ankle…how any one of those folds, sequences, waves has its own tone…qualities…each a little different. So that the contact and that the space around you is part of the shaping. […]the river across the top of the foot, the flow into the depth of the eye so that each eye finds a deep inner curvature in which to rest the retina, taking the inner self, the part of the brain that sees the world, back into itself, into the gyri of the floating brain, soft, full of deep clefts and inner folding.

See what folds of the joints seem to call your attention – shoulders, hip joints, ankles – and slowly begin to explore a bit of folding and unfolding – spiraling, sliding, the easiest pathway that emerges. What of your larger surfaces call to you, not feeling the need to finish any line, maybe the smallest movement of a fold dissolves into something else – no need to take a preconceived pathway, an extension or range of the fold and unfold. Let it carve itself into some other recess of you.

[…] You're a sheet that is shaping but not making shapes, the paradox of something flat and something curved, the emotional binding that speaks of continuity and discontinuity, that tailbone, that spine from its origins, liquid into substance, flat into fullness.

[…] knowing that the fold of the floor is coming to meet you as you come away from it, knowing moments of poise, rest, suspension, ease, letting go. Clarity, muddiness – and the interface between these.

[…] As you are finding your ways into alternate shapes, alternate sides, your orientation becomes anywhere. You celebrate that difference that emerges, the not knowing where, but the presence in the absence of deliberate orientation. The inner floating transfiguring, transforming…

[…] We started with the idea that folds are everywhere, the larger macro 'outside' of us and the folding into the micro of us. Eventually, the micro landscape of us emerges. The outer gains access to the inner in shaping and change of shaping, continuous, ongoing…

Notes

1. Somatic…. meaning

   The authors drew upon the legacy of Somatics (somatic education) with the aim of going beyond traditional approaches to training performative dance skills. Hallmarks of Somatics include augmenting sensory awareness and novelty in the use of language that fosters autonomous body/movement exploration and inquiry. Traditional approaches to dance improvisation, for example, focussed more on design elements than on exploring human corporeality (Eddy, 2016). Somatics broke through these older forms of training, offering a more emancipatory pedagogy free from mimicry- and mirror-based learning. Originally, Somatics forged a new paradigm of health and well-being, viewing the human body as the key resource in ownership, autonomy and agency (Hanna, 1970). As such, somatic education was touted as a living philosophy, growing its practices alongside phenomenological theory. Somatics is, at once, an ontology (the ways and means of being and coming into being) and an epistemology (knowledge gained by and through the body). Ontologically, the somatic processes that give rise to the infinite capability of the body for dramatic expression. The latter term refers more to the compendium of knowledge, the 'body' of knowledge, compiled through more than a century of dialogue between dance and mind-body (bodymind?) disciplines (Eddy, 2016). In line with the idea of freeing a body from its cultural habits and constraints or perhaps the habits/defaults or specificities of form/style that can restrict learning/exploring/experiencing, somatically based dance pedagogy aims at building autonomous dancers and avoids training a particular ideal body or specific identity. Somatic pedagogy emphasises more of an open, somatic play that would not only allow greater creativity but also hone in on each person's individuality, yielding not a 'defined' identity but one that is fluid and responsive through time and space. Best to start with the body, the process – we open a place for fluid, open experience to explore whatever palette.

2. Soma… meaning

   The word 'soma' comes from the ancient Greek meaning the totality of the human body. It was popularized explicitly by Dr Thomas Hanna in developing his concept of Somatics, a field of bodymind education. (See Note 1.) By 'soma', Hanna meant 'the body perceived from within' (https://somatics.org/library/htl-wis1).

'A soma is any individual embodiment of a process, which endures and adapts through time, and it remains a soma as long as it lives. The moment that it dies, it ceases to become a soma and becomes a body' (Hanna 1970: 31). Hanna, Thomas (1970), 'The Field of Somatics', *Somatics Magazine – Journal of the Bodily Arts and Sciences*, 1:1, pp. 30–34. Hanna's initial ideas generated a whole field of psychophysical education in which "the body is perceived as *the* source of human intelligence - one learns through the living body. It is exactly because the soma is alive and conscious that it can remember experiences as well as respond with awareness to life events...Somatic education assumes that humans are self-regulating and recognizes that the process of self-regulation is often overridden by thoughts and lifestyle practices".

(Martha Eddy, 2016, pp. 7–8)

Eddy, Martha (2016). *Mindful Movement: The Evolution of the Somatic Arts and Conscious Action*. Chicago, IL: University of Chicago Press.

References

Barthes, R. (1981). *Camera Lucida*. New York: Hill and Wang.

Batson, G. (2017). "Human origami: the embryo as a folding life continuum". *International Journal of Prenatal and Life Sciences*, 1(1), 1–20.

Bernard, M. (2001). *Creation Choreographique (RECHERCHES)*. Pantin, France: Centre National de la Danse.

Bresler, L. (Ed.) (2004). "Knowing bodies, moving minds: towards embodied teaching and learning", in *Landscapes: The Arts, Aesthetics, and Education*. Dordrecht, The Netherlands: Springer Science.

Chatterjee, A. (2017). "Of corporeal rewritings, translations, and the politics of difference in dancing", in R.J. Kowal, G. Siegmund, and R. Martin (Eds.), *The Oxford Handbook of Dance and Politics*. New York: Oxford University Press.

Chiesa, L. (2012). "A theatre of subtractive extinction: Bene without Deleuze", in I. Cull (Ed.), *Deleuze and Performance*. Edinburgh, Scotland: Edinburgh Scholarship Online.

Colebrook, C. (2005). "How can we tell the dancer from the dance: the subject of dance and the subject of philosophy". *Topoi*, 24(1), 5–14.

Cooper-Albright, A. (2013). *Engaging Bodies: The Politics and Poetics of Corporeality*. Middletown, CT: Wesleyan University Press.

Cooper-Albright, A. (2017). "Split intimacies: corporeality in contemporary theater and dance". *Choros International Dance Journal*, 6, 57–67.

Deleuze, G. (1993). *The Fold: Leibniz and the Baroque*. Minneapolis, MN: Regents of the University of Minnesota.

Deleuze, G. (1993). "One Manifesto Less", in CV Boundas (Ed.), A Orenstein (Trans), *The Deleuze Reader*. New York: Columbia University Press, USA.

Eddy, M. (2016). *Mindful Movement: The Evolution of the Somatic Arts and Conscious Action*. Chicago, IL: University of Chicago Press.

Foster, S.L. (1996). *Corporealities: Dancing Knowledge, Culture and Power.* London, UK: Routledge.

Hanna, T. (1970). "The field of Somatics". *Somatics Magazine – Journal of the Bodily Arts and Sciences*, 1(1), 30–34.

Hughes, J. (2017). "Pity the meat? Deleuze and the body", in L. Guillaume and J. Hughes (Eds.), *Deleuze and the Body.* Edinburgh, ST: Edinburgh University Press, pp. 1–6.

Manning, E. (2007). *Politics of Touch: Sense, Movement, Sovereign.* Minneapolis, MN: University of Minnesota.

Manning, E. (2009). *Relationscapes: Movement, Art, Philosophy (Technologies of Lived Abstraction).* Cambridge, MA: MIT Press.

O'Neill, C. (2015). "The epigenetics of embryo development". *Animal Frontiers I*, 5, 42–49.

Roche, J. (2015). "Dancing strategies and moving identities: the contributions independent contemporary dancers make to the choreographic process", in J. Butterworth and I. Wildschut (Eds.), *Contemporary Choreography: A Critical Reader.* Second Edition. London, UK: Routledge, pp. 150–165.

Sentler, S. (2019) in Lushetich, N. (Ed.) "The liquid architecture of bodily folding", in *Beyond Mind: Symbolism 2019, an Interdisciplinary Journal of Critical Aesthetics.* Boston/Berlin: De Gruyter Publications, pp. 137–148.

Sheets-Johnstone, M. (2012). *From Movement to Dance. Phenomenology and the Cognitive Sciences.* The Netherlands: Springer.

Smith, M. and Roche, J. (2015). "Perceiving the interactive body in dance: enhancing kinesthetic empathy through art objects". *Body, Space & Technology*, 14, doi: 10.16995/bst.35.

Williamson, A. (2010). 'Reflections and theoretical approaches to the study of spiritualities within the field of somatic movement dance education'. *Journal of Dance and Somatic Practices*, 2(1), 35–61.

4 *Shadowear*: a new way of re-(a)dressing the body

(Singapore)

Dinu C.T. Bodiciu

In search of a new paradigm

For centuries, the physical body has stood as the central denominator for garment construction and design. A three-dimensional entity with curves and slopes, under a continuous state of change and always in demand of new standards, the body has always challenged our creativity to reinvent and reinterpret season by season the same old fashions and styles. Blinded by its three-dimensionality, designers dealing with dressing, covering, protecting and embellishing it have always looked into its immediate corporeal features and functions. Conventional approaches to garment making have focussed on what is real and physical about a body, overlooking other features that the body is producing while interacting with the environment in which exists. I call these features extensions (from physical traces, like droppings, odours and vapours, to imprints onto surfaces, impalpable shadows, sounds, etc.), and I am interested in exploring how these extensions are influencing our understanding of what a body actually is and what it involves.

It is notable to mention that some forward-thinking artists have tackled the concept of expanding the body, both in analogue and digital fields. Artists like Rebecca Horn and Ann Hamilton are proposing a range of dress artefacts and extensions to enhance the body both physically and sensorially (Schwartzman, 2011). Orlan's practice of modifying the body in order to challenge norms of beauty is proposing a body in a continuous state of change, able to be stretched to unexpected limits. This body is actively living and organically responding to the society it lives in (Zylinska, 2002; Schwartzman, 2011). Taking a more sculptural approach, Caroline Broadhead is shifting attention from the body to the garment. Her early works, like *Ready to Wear* (1998), *Shadow Dress* and *Over My Shoulder (Yellow)* (1996), are attempts to give life to garments through the use of shadows.

Similarly, in the field of fashion, some designers have re-interpreted and challenged the body in various ways (Granata, 2017), questioning what garments are and how they can be worn, how garments are constructed and what they mean at a symbolic level as well as examining notions of beauty and perfection. For Rei Kawakubo and Yohji Yamamoto, the garment does not obey the volumes of the body: it actually challenges this body through distortions and volume shifts, almost as in a continuous search for a new physical identity. In Georgina Godfrey's designs the body becomes an object to be re-considered in an attempt to critically challenge norms of beauty and aesthetic, while for Martin Margiela the garment and implicitly the body are becoming the subject of dissection-like approaches in a search for the hidden social and cultural connotative data embedded within (Granata, 2017). In the above-mentioned examples where the garments have a double role – to dress a body and also to modify it while being dressed – the wearer becomes what Tarryn Handcock (2014) defines as a *skin that wears.* These attempts belong to the field of speculation where established notions of dress are invested with new semiotic values, challenging us to imagine matching garments for the various situations, contingencies and contexts in which a body could operate.

Further, I will briefly discuss two existing fashion practices, developed by labels such as Maison Martin Margiela (Spring/Summer 2011 collection) and Comme des Garçons (Fall/Winter 2012 collection), that attempted to challenge the three-dimensional body and imbued a flattened look through intricate construction approaches. Maison Martin Margiela's 2011 collection is an attempt to flatten the human body, at least at a first glance. By using engineered panelling and construction support materials, the designers have pushed most of the garment details to the front of the body onto the flattened textile surface, which becomes the only visible side of the garment when the subject is seen from the front. This attempt seems to challenge the perception of the body by generating a split between the head and limbs, which are left uncovered as three-dimensional appendices of a torso reduced to a geometric flat surface while it is depleted of any traces of organic nature.

For the Fall/Winter 2012 collection the Japanese brand Comme des Garçons proposed an exaggerated silhouette in an attempt to tackle canons about body size and proportions (Granata, 2016). The main fabric of each garment was transformed into a 'canvas' on which stylised silhouettes of the same design, but on a smaller scale, were pasted on, investing the entire look with a flat-like quality. While the flattened silhouette produced an oversized appearance, a vibrant colour palette was used to instil a buffoon-like appearance, accentuated by the exaggerated disproportion between the augmented garments and the small human parts appearing from behind them.

Although in both examples the three-dimensionality of the body has been considerably toned down, and the resulted designs permeate a flat-like appearance, neither of the approaches aimed to propose a new method for challenging the body and its extensions in the process of garment design. This design process still follows the rules of established fashion making paradigms: for instance consideration of construction, shape, fit and sizing. It is essential to note that in both examples the body, as a physical entity, still remains the reference for the entire garment construction and design process.

Through the method articulated in this chapter, I propose the expansion of the borders of identification of the body and implicit of the garments beyond the physical dimension into the territory of shadows, where the flatness of the projected body dissolves perceptions of race, size, individuality, gender and identity. As Stoichita (1997) argues, through the shadow, the identity of the individual is reduced to an *index*, where the mark of the body becomes a trace of its existence as a species. Taking this consideration as a premise, this research aims to render a new method for garment design as an alternative to current fashion design practices. Subsequently, this new method shifts the existing paradigms of benchmarking bodies into standards. Ultimately, this method is an attempt to stretch the boundaries of fashion beyond the confines of culturally and socially accepted approaches towards the body. It proposes instead a posthumanist perspective (Braidotti, 2013) by shifting the focus from the body to a more complex field of representation that takes into account the interaction between body and environment.

The shadow in culture and time

Although the anthropological apparatus conferring value and meaning to the shadow varies depending on culture and time, some indisputable traits could be attributed when considering an overall understanding of what shadows represent at a symbolic level.

Pliny's story in *Natural History, XXXV*, which recounts how Butades's daughter captured her lover's shadow by marking its outline on the wall, is the first record to document the origin of visual representation. As Stoichita (1997) highlights, the shadow becomes 'the other' of the physical body, reducing its identity to an appearance. Furthermore, the story tells us that Butades used the shadow's outline to sculpt the semblance of his daughter's loved one after the young man's death and that this sculpture was later kept in the temple at Corinth (Stoichita, 1997). With the help of this story we learn about the potential value of the shadow to be understood as the soul of the individual and that, upon the disappearance of the physical body, the soul (the double) could be kept alive through the sculpted representations (a double).

In addition to this premise, the Platonic scenario of the cave brings forth a new order of representation and exegesis whereby the realm of the shadow becomes alterity, reinforced and supported by the addition of sound (Stoichita, 1997). Strongly embedded in Plato's philosophy, "the shadow represents the stage that is furthest away from the truth" (Stoichita, 1997, p. 110) but also gains a fundamental semiotic charge, which prevails in the history of visual representation, being the semblance produced by the lack of light.

The role of the shadow as abstraction agent in the process of representation is vital for visual communication, as is distinguishable in the artistic expression of the shadow theatres around the world. In the Javanese art of *Wayang Kulit* (Chen, 2003; Korsovitis, 2003), where the *kelir* (the shadow projection screen symbolising the universe) becomes the meeting point of two worlds, the realm of gods and the realm of humans, the *dhalang* (puppeteer) is the agent (medium) making this intersection possible. Brandon (1993, p. 3; quoted by Chen, 2003, pp. 32–33) observes that spectators of the Wayang, although they know that what they see are just leather-carved and manipulated characters behind a canvas screen, "live in a world of illusions; they do not realise the magic hallucinations they see are not real". This observation becomes an important element in the construction of this methodology: namely, as the abstracted shadow becomes the source of imagination for the spectator, it becomes the trigger of a creative response in the design practice.

Furthermore, Piaget's work in setting up the framework for human cognitive development introduces the concept of the *shadow stage* (Piaget and Inhelder, 1956), which is further developed by Lacan in relation to the differentiation of the 'self' from the 'other'. As Lacan states, the *mirror stage* involves the identification of the '*I*', while the *shadow stage* involves the identification of the '*other*' (Lacan, 2006).

The shadow as a mediator of a new design approach

I would like to further outline the important role played by the shadow as a mediator in the cognitive apparatus of identification. As Victor Stoichita argues (1997), the shadow could be seen as a conversion agent from particular (the *I*, the individual) to general (the *other*, the common), preserving the confines of the species but lacking details about race, size, identity and even gender. The shadow becomes the *Index* (Stoichita, 1997) of the species, a territory which has been cleared of any traces of individuality. Following this line of thought, bringing the subject to this level of abstraction (a shadow) will allow the receptor (the designer) to imagine features beyond the confines of reality, thus becoming a new tool for ideation and an alternative space yet to be explored for fashion design.

Based on these considerations I am proposing the following speculative design approach (Dunne and Raby, 2013) as an innovative conceptualisation process, illustrated below (Figure 4.1), which delineates the thought process used as the instigator of a practical design methodology. The translation of the three-dimensional data of a body into the flat surface of its casted shadow could be seen as a process of *abstraction* in which the individual features of the subject have disappeared. The shadow becomes an intermediary state, a converter, whereby only a set of basic information about the body has been kept and will be further used for the process of *ideation* of new elements of dress.

I will detail the practical methodology of addressing the shadow from the perspective of garment design and production, which entails three main stages:

Stage 1: Abstraction (Production and recording of the shadow)
Stage 2: Translation – Ideation
Stage 3: Making

Shifting the focus of the designer/garment-maker from the three-dimensionality of the body (which brings forth considerations about measurements) to the flatness of the shadow replaces the rigorous set of data, as required by traditional methods of garment production, with a simple rule: the narrowest section of the shadow has to fit the

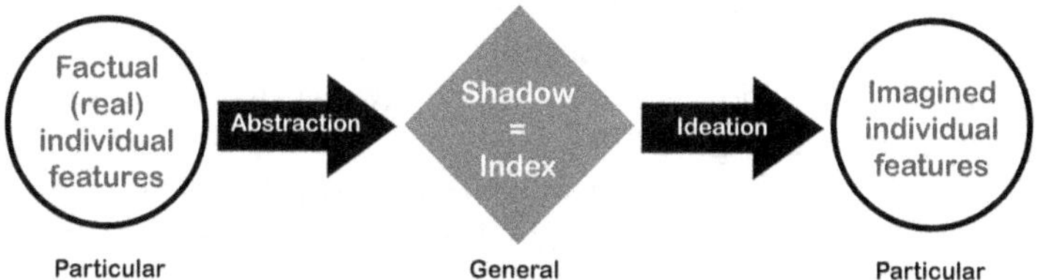

Figure 4.1 Diagram illustrating the conceptualisation process which grounds the *Shadowear* design method. Photographer: Dinu C.T. Bodiciu.

respective part of the body it corresponds to. For a clear understanding of the proposed method a series of illustrations and visual documentation gathered during my own practice will be used.

Stage 1: Abstraction (production and recording of the shadow)

The first stage in the process, which is of the utmost importance in capturing a body's shadow as the subject for subsequent stages, is the documentation of the shadow. As a transient extension of the body, and in a continuous change, the shadow is always influenced by some physical and optical parameters: the source of light, the distance between the source of light and the subject, the surface the shadow is projected on and the angle of projection. The combination of these parameters influences the shadows' intensity, shape, size, proportions and distortion ratio, thus influencing the process of abstraction of the body.

There are two main sources of light: natural (sun, moon, fire) orartificial (incandescent light, fluorescent light), each one producing a particular type of shadow. Although the source of light is the most important factor in the production of the shadow – and with technological developments, the types of artificial light have strongly diversified – the source of light only influences the intensity of the shadow (the light-dark contrast between the shadow and the surrounding), and it will not be further considered in this research. As this method benefits only from the shape and distortion of the shadow, the following three factors are most relevant and will be further studied.

The distance between the source of light and the body is the factor responsible for the size of the shadow. There is a simple rule, which has been used since the 14th century and documented by artists like Alberti, Leonardo and Durer (Stoichita, 1997): namely that the size of the projected shadow is inverse proportional with the distance between the source of light and the subject. For shadows cast under light originating from astral bodies like the sun and the moon (Figure 4.2a), the size of the shadow is close to the actual size of the body (not yet considering the angle of projection, which will be detailed later), whereas if the shadow is produced by an artificial source like a candle or a lightbulb, positioned close to the body, the shadow will become augmented in size (Figure 4.2b).

The third aspect is the angle of projection which influences the proportions of the shadow, specifically the harmony between length and width. The wider the angle between the source of light and the shadows' projection surface, the bigger the proportion between the length and the width of the shadow will be. This angle could range from 90 to

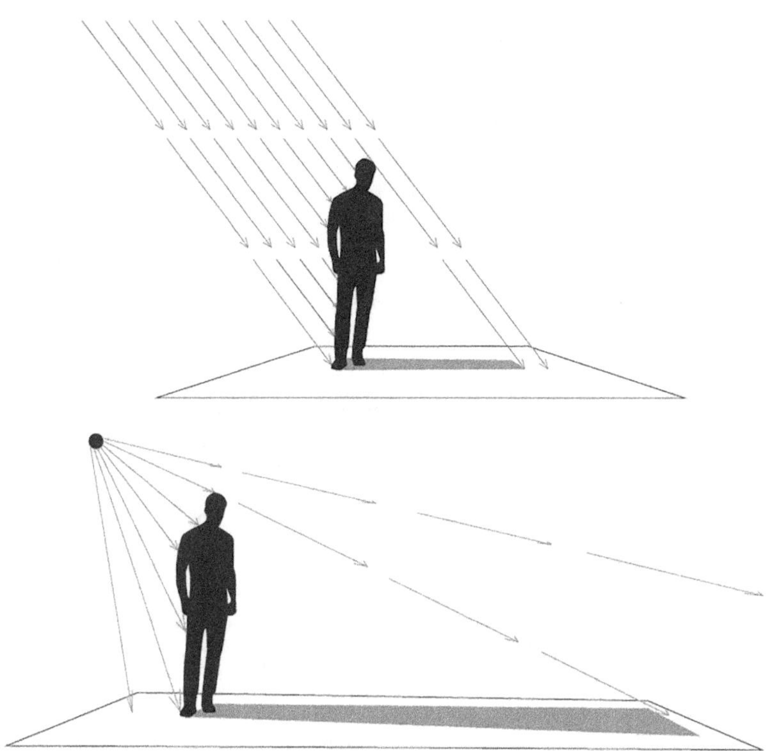

Figure 4.2 (a) Shadow produced by astral bodies. (b) Shadow produced by artificial light. Photographer: Dinu C.T. Bodiciu.

180 degrees (see below Figure 4.3a and 4.3b, which showcase this relation). A clear example would be the difference in shadow lengths produced by the sun at two distinct times of day. At one end, noon, when the angle of projection is closer to 90 degrees, the shadow is the shortest, sometimes hidden under our feet. At the other end, sunset, when the angle of projection is closer to 180 degrees, the length of the shadow could appear stretched for meters, even dissolving into the horizon.

The surface of projection is the fourth aspect to be considered in generating a shadow. If the projection is produced on a flat surface, the outline of the shadow will be smooth in contrast with a more textured projection surface (objects, shapes), where the shadow will be distorted (Figure 4.4). Together with the angle of projection, this aspect is responsible for the distortion of the shadow.

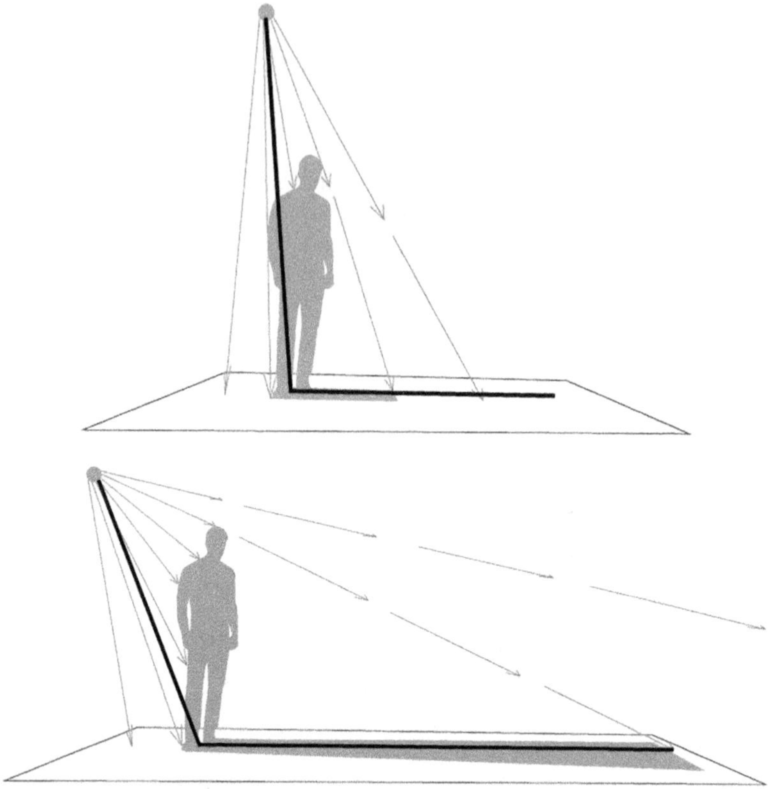

Figure 4.3 (a) Shadow produced at an angle of 93 degrees. (b) Shadow produced at an angle of 115 degrees. Photographer: Dinu C.T. Bodiciu.

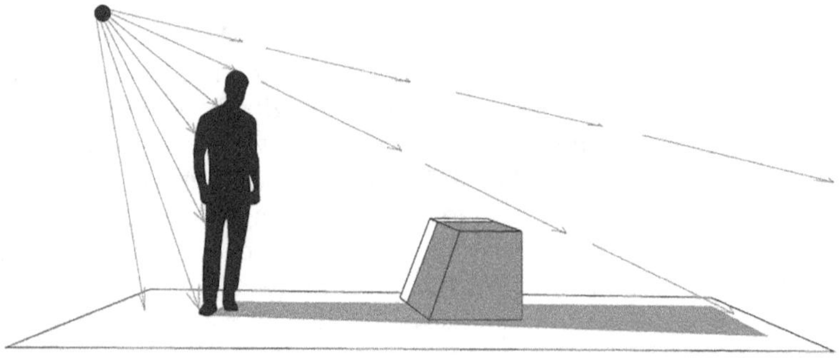

Figure 4.4 Illustration showcasing the distortion of the shadow when projected on textured surfaces. Photographer: Dinu C.T. Bodiciu.

Utilising the interrelation between these four parameters, the resulting shadow could be strongly controlled and anticipated in order to serve as a suitable starting point for this design method. As shadow itself is the catalyst of the creative process, it becomes the main apparatus that designers can explore with when undertaking this method.

Stage 2: Translation – ideation

Once the desired shadow has been achieved and photographed, through the process of translation – ideation, a new item of dress will be conceptualised. The photographed shadow, although it lacks most of the details of the subject which has produced it, as discussed earlier, maintains certain traces of spatiality and body posture. Like an investigator, the designer will proceed with an imaginative reconstruction of the three-dimensionality of the body which produced the shadow. This process of reconstruction can be addressed as two-fold: in a rigorous manner, a process which I will name *translation*, when traces of dress recorded in the outline of the shadow are regenerated by the designer into new garments, or in a creative manner, a process which I will name *ideation*, when the silhouette of the shadow stands only as a canvas, and the designer has the liberty to design garments beyond the confines of the shadow and without any reference to the shadowy traces of the garments worn by the subject which generated the shadow.

By approaching the process of *translation*, the designer will act as an *investigator* (Figure 4.7), trying to elucidate elements of dress worn by the subject when the shadow was documented. Through *translation*, the surface of the shadow is the boundary within which the designer can creatively express by tracing details of construction and features for the new imagined garment. Although this process seems quite restrictive there remains a wide area of exploration which allows the design process to cross beyond the reiteration of archetypal garment details and features (Figure 4.5a–c).

Compared with *translation*, the second approach, *ideation* (Figure 4.6a–d), imposes no restrictions, allowing the designer to manifest freely as a *creator* (Figure 4.7) while addressing the shadow only as a reference for the pose or spatiality for the newly designed garment and as a source of data regarding fit and wear. This approach challenges the designer to reconcile established notions and knowledge about garment construction and detailing in contrast with innovative, accidental and progressive interpretations of what elements of dress and fashion may become.

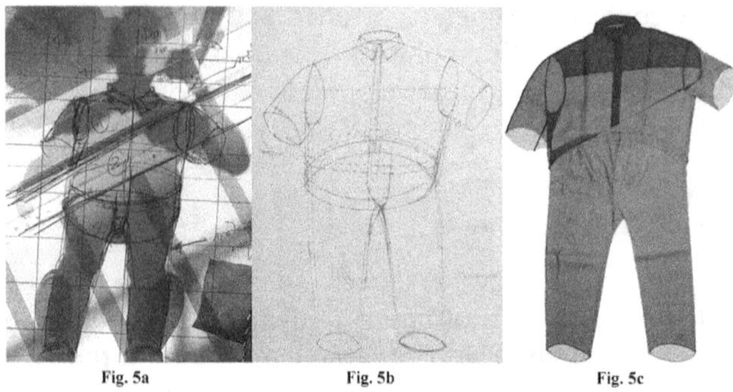

Figure 4.5 Translation approach illustrated as (a) Shadow. (b) Intermediary pattern. (c) Final garment. Photographer: Dinu C.T. Bodiciu.

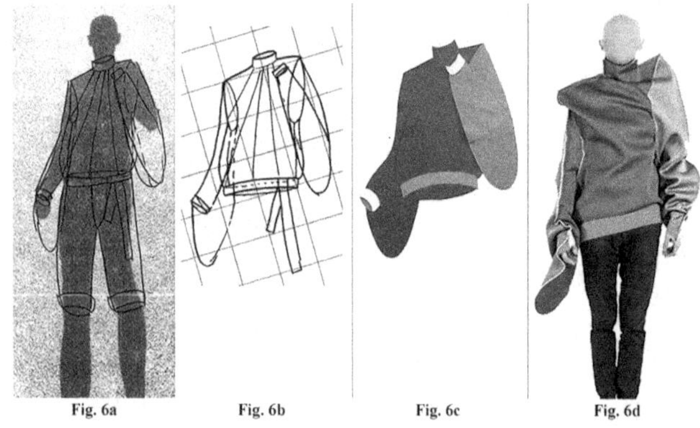

Figure 4.6 Ideation approach illustrated (a) As shadow. (b) The intermediary design on a grid. (c) Final garment as flat. (d) On a three-dimensional body.

Regardless of approach (translation or ideation) this stage requires a strong understanding of spatiality and tri-dimensional representation in flat. As both approaches open up a boundless territory where speculation and experimentation can be exercised, in terms of fashion design and construction knowledge, this remains the most demanding stage of this method.

Stage 3: Making

Once the new design has been completed, the sketch will be brought through scaling to a size suitable for the body. Although for the development of this research I have used a grid (Figure 4.6b) as a technical tool for rendering the designed garment to body size, a wide range of analogue and digital scaling methods could be used as well. The scaled design will be further drafted and cut in the desired material(s). There is only one rule about measurements when scaling the design to human-size: the narrowest section of the shadow (and implicitly of the newly designed garment) has to fit the body area to which it corresponds when the garment is dressed. If this rule is followed the garment will always fit the body that it has been designed for.

It is important to outline that from the drafting stage each piece of a pattern is different than the other, unlike in the traditional garment-making processes, where most of the time the majority of the panels are cut in pairs, given the symmetric nature of the body. For this method the pattern pieces and the assembling process becomes similar to a puzzle game, involving the maker's attention and logic. As this design method does not cater to mass production or a fast fashion practice, given the intricacy of the assembling and sewing process, a close dialogue between the designer and the maker is advisable. In terms of fabric waste production, given the complexity of the patterns a strong consideration for minimising unused space when generating the lay-plan is required.

Other key aspects strongly contributing to the final fit and drape of the garment are the fabrics and construction materials used. Following traditional fabric choices or going against the norm are choices that designers should consider in order to achieve the desired level of novelty in the final outcome. For example, when making a classic jacket, in addition to the main fabrics a whole range of construction materials, like interfacing, canvas, felt, padding and assembly knowledge, is required, whilst in the case of *Shadowear* making, all this knowledge is challenged and, even more, could be fully eradicated. The accidental ways in which the garment will drape on the body as a result of all these material considerations is the most important outcome of this method, positioning the designer in a new role, as a *spectator*, discovering unexpected features of his own work (Figure 4.7). Given that this method renders a new approach for design, the choice and combination of materials and production methods could also be the subject of further consideration as it opens new territory for design investigation.

The final outcome – the new 'shadow' garment – carries a series of features, investing the design with intangible values that contrast with those of traditionally produced garments, such as some characteristic features of the original subject, from pose, to body attitude and setting context. These features, together with details added through the design

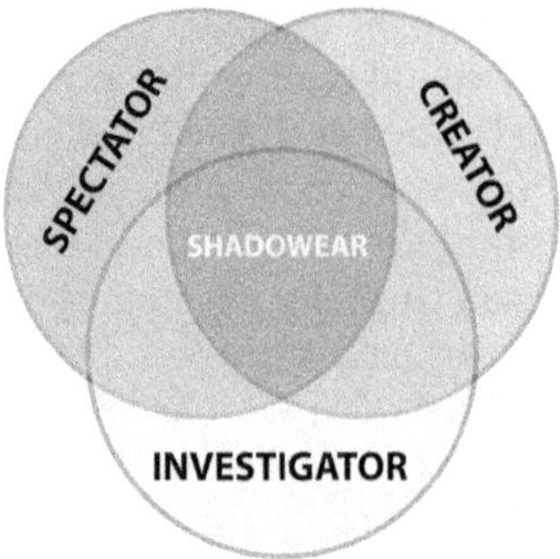

Figure 4.7 A diagram which illustrates how the combination of the three roles played by the designer as an investigator, creator and spectator are contributing together when undertaking the *Shadowear* method. Photographer: Dinu C.T. Bodiciu.

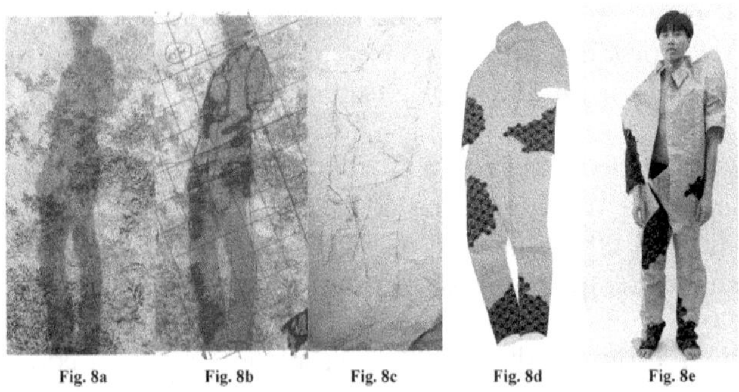

Figure 4.8 Illustrations of the entire *Shadowear* method, from abstraction through translation/ideation and the making of the new garment. (a) The original shadow. (b) The translation of the garment using the grid. (c) The scaled design. (d) The final garment on a flat surface. (e) The final garment on a three-dimensional body. Photographer: Dinu C.T. Bodiciu.

process, instil the new garment with an aura of complexity which invites the receptor to decode the design language and its aims in a completely new light by shifting the paradigm of knowledge on the relation between body and garment into a new territory (Figure 4.8a–e). This new territory can be articulated based on the post-structuralist concept of the 'line-of-flight' proposed by Deleuze and Guattari (1987). Thus, I take the new relationship between the body and the garments designed through this new method as articulating a line of flight, that is, a system and process of semiosis which reaches a maximum of centrifugal energy and escapes a given territory of traditional garments knowledge and representation to rearticulate itself in the territory of significance of the *Shadowear*. Through this process, *Shadowear* will open new meanings in relation to concepts of dress as a cultural construct and of the relationship between the body and the garment as new territories to be populated with semiotic content.

Conclusion

The above-detailed *Shadowear* method opens up new strands for fashion design practice. By shifting the designer's attention from the physical subject to the body's shadow as the *index,* the entire process of the design and construction of garments is filtered through an apparatus similar to a process of 'unknowing' (Hara, 2015).

This method casts a new light on understanding the body and identity while giving substance to a quotidian and daily existence, and bringing forth awareness about what we are as entities beyond the confines of a physical body. Stretching the body past the boundaries of familiar human representation set by traditional fashion design and production paradigms obscures the prototypical model of the Vitruvian man towards a posthumanist framework.

The innovative side of this method could be articulated as a three-pronged approach, with benefits for both the designer and the wearer as direct participants in this process as well as for the enrichment of the design language from cultural and social perspectives.

From the perspective of the designer/maker, the method broadens the complexity of roles invested in by the designer, from creator to investigator and spectator. By handling a wider range of roles, the designer becomes an agile and versatile player when developing a practice and conveying a message.

On the wearer side, this method challenges archetypal notions about garments and dress codes. The wearer is faced with products which carry clear and recognisable traces of known elements of dress, while they are flat and not worn. The minute these garments are dressed, the expected appearance is shifted to a distorted reality which pushes the subject into an uncomfortable and disruptive angle, allowing a wider field for play, exploration and a re-evaluation of what 'dressed' and 'dressing' could entail.

Finally, *Shadowear* can be considered as a teaching approach for fashion design, instigating critical thinking and combining, in a fluid and dynamic manner, creative and technical processes with investing a thorough knowledge of fashion history and construction and simultaneously challenging it.

References

Bolton, A. (2011). *Rei Kawakubo/Comme des Garcons: Art of the In-Between.* New York: The Metropolitan Museum of Art, p. 127.

Braidotti, R. (2013). *The Posthuman.* Cambridge: Polity.

Brandon, J. R. (1993). *On Thrones of Gold: Three Javanese Shadow Plays.* Honolulu: University of Hawai'i Press, pp. 1–3.

Chen, F. P. (2003). 'Shadow Theaters of the World", *Asian Folklore Studies*, Vol. 62, No. 1, pp. 25–64.

Deleuze, G. and Guattari, F. (1987). *A Thousand Plateaus: Capitalism and Schizophrenia.* Minneapolis: University of Minnesota Press, pp. 123–164.

Dunne, A. and Raby, F. (2013). *Speculative Everything; Design, Fiction and Social Dreaming.* Cambridge, MA: The MIT Press.

Granata, F. (2016). "Mikhail Bakhtin: Fashioning the Grotesque Body", in A. Rocamora and A. Smelik (eds.), *Thinking through Fashion*, 1st ed. London: I.B. Tauris, pp. 97–114.

Granata, F. (2017). *Experimental Fashion: Performance Art, Carnival and the Grotesque Body.* London: I.B. Tauris.

Handcock, T. (2014). *Skin That Wears: Body-Site as a Context for Designing Wearable Artefacts.* [pdf]. Melbourne: RMIT University. Available at https://researchbank.rmit.edu.au/view/rmit:161236 [Accessed 3 February 2018].

Hara, K. (2015). *Ex-formation.* Zurich: Lars Muller Publishers, pp. 8–20.

Korsovitis, C. (2013). "Ways of the Wayang", *The Everyday The Familiar and THE BIZARRE, India International Centre Quarterly*, Vol. 28, No. 2, pp. 59–68.

Lacan, J. (2006). "The Mirror Stage as Formative of the I Function as Revealed in Psychoanalytic Experience", *Écrits: The First Complete Edition in English* [trans. Bruce Fink]. New York: W.W. Norton and Company.

Piaget, J. and Inhelder, B. (1956). *A Child's Conception of Space.* London: Routledge & K. Paul.

Schwartzman, M. (2011). *See Yourself Sensing: Redefining Human Perception.* London: Black Dog Publishing.

Stoichita, V. I. (1997). *A Short History of the Shadow.* London: Reaktion Books Ltd.

Zylinska, J. (2002). *The Cyborg Experiments: The Extensions of the Body in the Media Age.* London: Continuum.

5 Water is Never Still: Araya Rasdjarmrearnsook's sculptural and installation practice[1]

(Thailand)

Clare Veal

The sea is dark and wide, the sky peppered with white clouds. The female figure's male companion is perched in front of her, his long tail penetrating the frame that dictates her view. She stares beyond him to an ocean found between disembodied legs, splayed wide. Night comes, and the male bird takes flight, in and out of the frame. Now that he has left, she can see the moon's reflection on the ocean. Submitting to his movements with open arms, her head is motionless, but the water is never still. *Isolated Moral Female Object, in a Relationship with a Male Bird I* and *II*, both made in 1995, represent characteristics that are paradigmatic of Araya Rasdjarmrearnsook's (b. 1957) installation and sculptural practice of the early and mid-1990s: disembodied body parts cast in plaster, androgynous heads with generic features and repurposed domestic furniture. In the 1990s, Araya's installations gained international and national acclaim, as indicated by her two solo shows at Thailand's National Gallery (1994 and 1995) and her inclusion in a number of major international exhibitions. This fact might be explained through these works' apparent convergence with the materiality and subject matter of other installations produced by Thai and South-East Asian artists working in this period.[2] More recently, attention to her practice has focussed on her video works, particularly those involving corpses, as indicating her transgressions of officially sanctioned taste in the Thai context.[3] The reception of Araya's works has thus ranged from celebration to 'hostility and derision', but these reactions cannot be entirely understood as related to her choice of medium.[4] Her early prints gained support and recognition through national prizes, while her installations and videos have been selected for exhibition by both Thai and foreign curators.[5] Meanwhile her work has been subject to criticism: for example in the 'miniature media storm' that arose in Thailand when Araya was awarded a national art

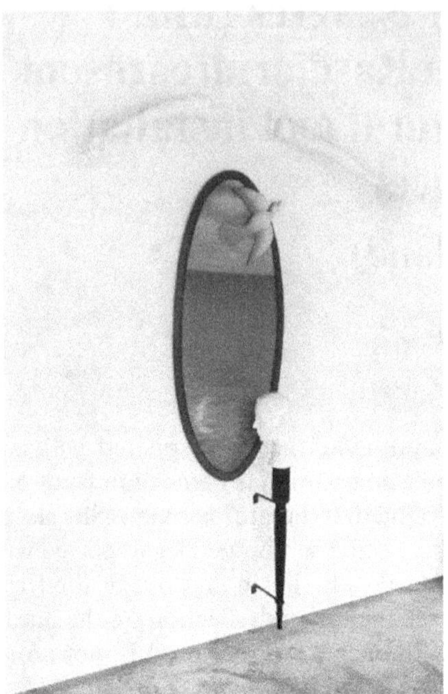

Figure 5.1 *Isolated Moral Female Object, in a Relationship with a Male Bird II* (1995). Araya Rasdjarmrearnsook. Mixed media, dimensions unknown. Collection of Jean Michel Beurdeley. Courtesy of the artist and 100 Tonson Gallery, Bangkok.

prize for a print work she made by copying a photograph as well as the many delays before she was belatedly awarded full professorship at Chiang Mai University (Figure 5.1).[6]

Because Araya's video works appear to more directly involve 'social realities', one might surmise that her practice developed in more radical ways after her movement from prints to installation in the early 1990s and then to video from 1997 onwards.[7] Yet transitional works, including a series of zinc plates produced in 1993, which were framed to emphasise their three-dimensionality and displayed with found objects, undermine clear distinctions between her two-dimensional and sculptural practices. Her later moving-image works are also imbued with a sense of spatial awareness. This is manifested through the scale or orientation of video projections; the characteristics of seating provided for viewers; and, more recently, the use of sculptural replications of figures from her moving-image works as a way to underline the porousness of the video frame. Referencing Araya's 2018 exhibition at 100

Tonson Gallery, Bangkok, entitled 'An Artist is Trying to Return to "Being a Writer"', May Adadol Ingawanij has related the 'untimeliness' of Araya's 'late style' to her 'intermedial' practice, which refuses 'resolution' in favour of 'intransigence, irreconcilability and lack of unity'.[8] This exhibition not only points to Araya's prolific writing practice in a range of genres (she produced a novel during the six-month period of the show) but also circumscribes a linear model of artistic development in favour of an anachronistic 'return'. In a move that is simultaneously kindred with and opposite to this, this chapter moves towards one of the artist's beginnings, not in the hope of returning to the origin of a chronological development but in an attempt to read its refractions through the insights gleaned from her subsequent practice.[9]

The water in the basin and the rush of the current

One clear way in which the various forms of Araya's practice reflect her intermedial approach is through their involvement of the qualities of movement and stasis. Her installations are large in scale and frequently utilise weathered materials that might appear as if they were unearthed from a distant past if it were not for the perfect manner in which they are deliberately distressed. In these works, stillness is equated with a state of constriction, and at times, it appears to become the physical realisation of a lack of agency. This is this same quality that Sayan Daengklom describes in his analysis of Araya's video *Conversation of Two Women* (1998), in which the artist recites to a female corpse passages from the classical Thai epic *Inao*, which is thought to be derived from the East Javanese Panji tales. Here, Sayan links a lack of movement to the qualities of coffins and the restrictions placed on femininity.[10] We can see affinities between Sayan's analysis and the disembodied limbs of *Isolated Hands Asking for Help* (1992) (Figure 5.2).

Here, plaster casts of the artist's lower arms appear paralysed and alone, their bent fingers anticipating an impossible movement. The black coffin-shaped basin that comprises their support is filled with motor oil (the reflective qualities of which are used to approximate still water), and this liquid appears to gradually dissolve these bodily forms.[11]

While earlier works like *Isolated Hands*, reflected a sense of solitary self-contemplation,[12] this quality of disembodiment was linked in Araya's later installations, produced after 1994, to the perceived limitations imposed by cultural expectations and socio-economic situations. More specifically, these works critically engaged with the conditions that inform the lives of Thai women as those the artist might herself identify with.[13] This apparent movement from a preoccupation with

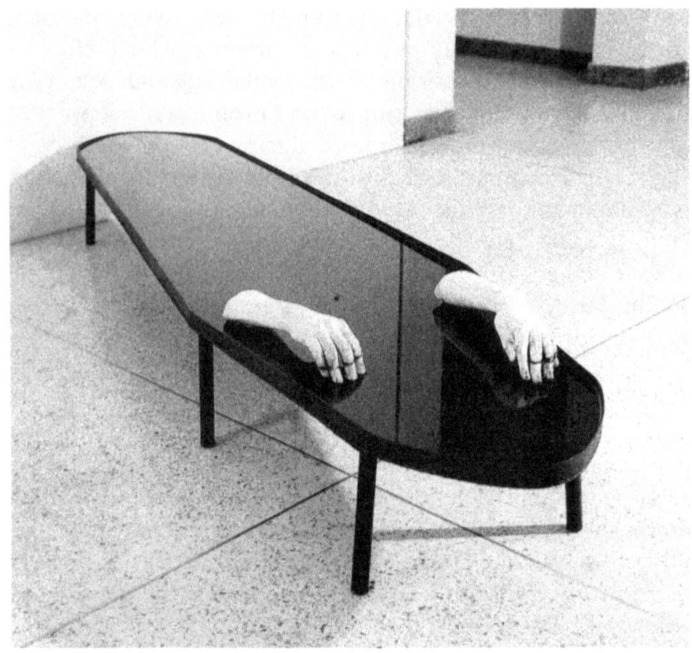

Figure 5.2 *Isolated Hands Asking for Help* (1992). Araya Rasdjarmrearnsook. Plaster, iron and motor oil. Courtesy of the artist and 100 Tonson Gallery, Bangkok.

the 'self' to an examination of the ways in which that 'self' might connect and empathise with others may have been prompted by a series of interviews that Araya conducted with Thai women migrant workers in Germany between 1988 and 1990, in which she discussed with her fellow 'countrywomen' the hardships they faced as housewives, waitresses, masseurs and sex workers.[14]

Araya's concern with the expectations and roles assigned to Thai women is exemplified in *Departure of Thai Country Girls* (1995), an installation that has been interpreted as representing the migration (or trafficking) of women from rural Thailand so they might be employed in the sex work industry.[15] In this work, pairs of upturned legs, carved from wood, are situated in a heavy structure similar to that of a boat. The blackened appearance of these body parts, analogous to charred corpses on a funeral pyre, makes reference to their lifeless nature. Meanwhile, the boat-like structure provides a frame within which they are caged. Yet this entrapment is made all the more menacing through references to the dangerous potentiality of what might exist beyond this

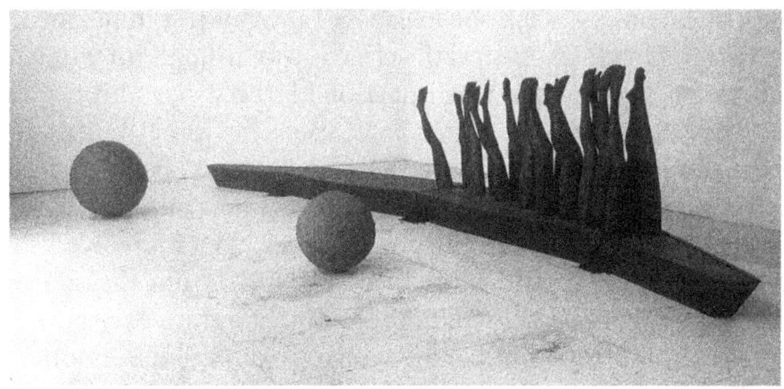

Figure 5.3 *Departure of Thai Country Girls* (1995). Araya Rasdjarmrearnsook. Wood, steel and charcoal, 700 x 100 cm. Collection of Jean Michel Beurdeley. Courtesy of the artist and 100 Tonson Gallery, Bangkok.

frame. As the wooden boat transports its cargo, black ashy powder leaks out from its joints, perhaps representing what happens to those who attempt to escape, their bodies disintegrating in the water (Figure 5.3).

My reading of *Departure* is informed by a series of short stories by Araya, which were written at the same time as her interviews undertaken in Germany and later published in the collection *Phuying Tawanok* [*Women of the East*, 1993].[16] One of these texts, '*Nam* [Water]', comprises a series of vignettes, described in vivid, sensorial detail, recounting scenes from a woman's childhood in Thailand, remembered as she takes a shower, far from home. Each of the joyful recollections – floating on a rubber ring in a river, playing in the mud or swimming in a pond in the hot sun – results in swift, negative outcomes: a close drowning or physical punishment from family members. The end of the story returns to a description of the shower, the woman curled in the corner, listening to the sound of water running down the drain. This is a sound that she never heard as a child, and now as an adult, far from home, it comes to represent a new experience. As in *Departure*, I understand water here as symbolising the lure of freedom as well as the potential danger in violating the limits of cultural expectations. Indeed, it seems that even water itself is shaped by the cultural readings given to it, the container into which it is poured.

When read in conjunction with Araya's installations, her text *Nam* complicates questions of movement and stasis, and their assumed relationships to freedom and constraint. Moreover, these qualities come to refer not only to issues of materiality but also to process. An understanding of sculpture as heavy and static can be related to its characterisation as 'masculine' in the Thai context. This was indicated in the negative reactions that Araya faced from her lecturers at Bangkok's Silpakorn University when she expressed her interest in the medium.[17] Their warnings that sculptural practice is too difficult for women were echoed in 2007, when she was questioned about her ability to make 'heavy' sculpture.[18] At the same time, speaking about her preference for three-dimensional practice in the mid-1990s, Araya contrasted the 'stillness' of producing two-dimensional works with the movement implicated in her construction of sculptures, which involved shifting her body's physical relationship with the work, from sitting down to standing up.[19] We have here a number of interpretative paradoxes that appear to problematise (reversing and replaying) the assumed correspondences between the binaries of masculinity/femininity, stasis/movement and heaviness/lightness.

As installations, these works not only involve the artist's body and the bodies of the disintegrated or absent figures that form her subject matter; they also implicate those of the audience within a particular type of intersubjective relationship. In determining how such a relationship might be characterised, the reactions of reviewers to Araya's installation *Buang* [*Trap*] (1995) – comprising of a number of precariously stacked objects surrounding a sculptural figure, whose head and legs jut out of a wooden basin that also contains the smashed remains of its torso – when it was exhibited in 1997 as part of the widely cited exhibition 'Contemporary Art in Asia: Traditions/Tensions', are particularly revealing.[20] Take, for instance, Lynne Cooke's review. She writes, "While death and loss lie at the heart of this work, no clear-cut elucidation of meaning was possible". Indeed, "the piece functioned through a telling juxtaposition of its various and often ambiguous components and through their tautly calibrated placement" (Figure 5.4).

Cooke's review was one of the few that treated *Buang* in any substantial detail, with many others choosing to mention only the figure in the wooden basin rather than the other 'ambiguous components' of the work: wooden planks positioned horizontally above the figure, a stone suspended from the ceiling, a screen comprised of dark X-ray images, metal plates with images of human bones mounted on the wall and a stack of charred logs. The fact that each of these elements is reliant on something else to stand up by itself seems to produce a sense of unease or even fear in the viewer/participant.[21] This was registered in Cooke's observation that the work forced audiences to make "uncomfortable decisions concerning whether, and if so how, one would enter the terrain mapped by the work".[22] It is as if any wrong move would set off a chain reaction, causing the tentatively stacked structures to collapse, crushing themselves and, perhaps, the body/bodies of the figure/artist/viewer.

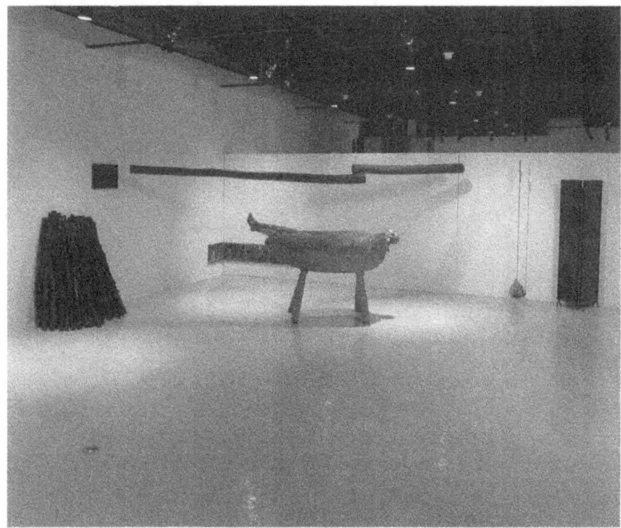

Figure 5.4 *Buang* [*Trap*] (1995). Araya Rasdjarmrearnsook. Wood, metal plates, stone, clay, fiberglass, dimensions variariable. Installation view, 'Contemporary Art in Asia: Traditions/Tensions', October-December 1996, organised by the Asia Society, New York. Courtesy of the artist and 100 Tonson Gallery, Bangkok.

Water is Never Still

The reluctance with which reviewers engaged with *Buang* was likely linked to its physical structure and the ways in which it rebuffed or reflected the audience that encountered it. We can draw analogies between this and Araya's use of reflective surfaces in other works of the same period. This includes her site-specific work displayed at Wat Umong as part of the 'Chiang Mai Social Installation: Third Art and Cultural Festival' (1995–1996), which comprised a mirrored box placed, as if floating, on a small pond. The stillness of the object would have reflected the movement of the audience as well as the fluctuations of the water that surrounded it. However, its environmental placement would have simultaneously circumscribed the audience's ability to move close to it. In photographs of this work, the box seems to disappear into the landscape, producing an optical illusion that might have compelled audience members to throw stones at it, destroying it and their own reflections.[23] Taken together, these installations produce a relationality that refuses coherency through artistic unveiling. Instead, they implicate the audience in ways that force them to place

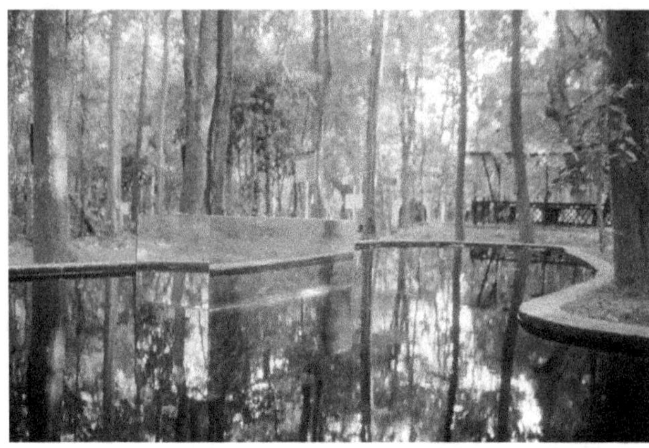

Figure 5.5 Untitled work installed at Wat Umong as part of the Chiang Mai Social Installation (1995–6). Araya Rasdjarmrearnsook. Courtesy of the artist and 100 Tonson Gallery, Bangkok. Photograph courtesy of Uthit Atimana and Gridthiya Gaweewong, CMSI Archive.

themselves in vulnerable situations, stuck between the unthinkable choice between remaining static or facing the threat of what might happen if one moves (Figure 5.5).

The manner in which these works simultaneously engaged and reflected their audiences might seem to situate Araya's installation practice in proximity to the sociopolitical aims of several Thai and South-East Asian artists working in installation during the same period, many of whom exhibited alongside her in shows such as 'Traditions/Tensions' and 'Chiang Mai Social Installation', among others.[24] For instance, Araya's adoption of 'local' materials – such as corn husks used by villagers in Northern Thailand to make funerary flowers, which were piled into the shape of a pyre in *Has the Girl Lost her Memory* (1994/2014) – appear to reflect what Julie Ewington posited as the 'congeniality' between installation and the 'indigenous cultural traditions of Southeast Asia'.[25] It is within such resonances, and their ability to reconfigure the relationship between artists and their publics, that Patrick D. Flores finds an artist's 'desire…to convene an art world, or a relational transpersonal world of art, by creating conditions for people to assemble along the various axes of dissent, development, nationalism and solidarity' (Figure 5.6).[26]

Yet, as we have seen, Araya's installations combine this invitation towards the 'collective' with the impossibility of accepting it, complicating the ways in which her works come to (or refuse to) speak to their publics. In an interview with the Thai artist Kamol Phaosavasdi,

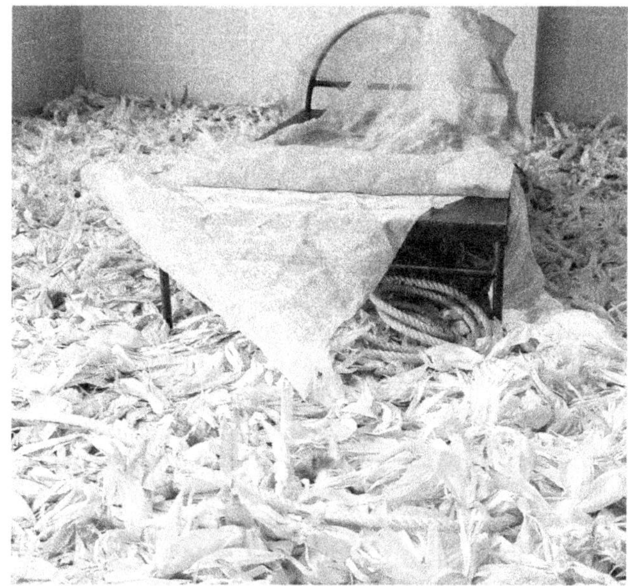

Figure 5.6 Has the Girl Lost her Memory 2 (1994). Araya Rasdjarmrearnsook. Courtesy of the artist and 100 Tonson Gallery, Bangkok.

printed in the catalogue for his 2001 exhibition 'Dilemma', Araya questions the relationship between the artist, their practice and their publics. On the one hand, she claims that the 'artist is someone uniquely positioned in our community to offer a critical perspective on our society'. Yet further questions arise as to how to apprehend and evaluate critical artistic practice from within the same social conditions that the works critique.[27] Moreover, as Araya enquires, what are the ethical responsibilities of artists whose works 'borrow' social issues to 'make their work more "meaningful", to demonstrate their "political responsibility"'? And who do such works address?[28] Implicit in Araya's questions is a critique regarding the artist's position as a political agent, the 'voice' of the people. As May Adadol Ingawanij has posited, Araya's late style demonstrates a 'studied scepticism regarding the social and political agency of artists and artworks'.[29] In particular, she notes Araya's awareness of the limitations of the leftist *Sinlapa Phuea Chiwit* [Art for Life] movement which emerged in Thailand during the Cold War and imagined the artist 'as part of a masculinist intellectual class in an underdeveloped society'.[30] For Araya, this artistic model entails a split between artists and the populations who they aim speak for/to.[31]

This cynical attitude that May identifies in Araya's later practice anachronistically informs my reading of her early installations in ways that un- and re-frame them as 'feminist' practice. This is not to repeat the contention that 'Western' feminism does not apply in the Thai context or to posit that Araya's installations do not speak to feminist issues when they clearly do.[32] However, following Jacques Derrida, it is to recognise the distinction between, and mutual imbrication of, a feminism based upon the progressivist 'liberation' of women and the possibility of stepping back into 'absolutely heterogeneous pockets, irreducible particularities, of unheard of and incalculable sexual differences'.[33] Of course, following the advice of Araya's father, as recounted by her, 'If you don't think of it as a choice between two things, then you can try to make both'.[34] This also means maintaining the possibilities of remaining still while moving; of being irreducibly singular while recognising the impossibility of speaking to/from that singularity without recourse to generalisations; and, finally, of seizing the empathetic and practical potential of adopting identificatory categories in the knowledge that these can be (and must be) un-formed in the future.[35]

In Araya's writings from the early 1990s, the status of the individual artist is often formulated as a space of freedom outside of the strictures of the cultural expectations that accompany one's identification as a member of a 'collective'. As she states,

> It is painful that we never make choices completely, boldly, directly and instantaneously. The connections both to corporeal individuals and intangible things, bind – fastened tightly with social values [...] Because this state can never be resolved, various restrictions thus play a role in my artworks....[36]

This may also explain Araya's reluctance to engage with identity politics within her practice. As she explained, "Individuality is something that I am searching for in artistic practice, by attempting to go on according to nature; according to the nature that I desire to realise for myself".[37] In fact, even when speaking about works, like *Buang*, that were curatorially framed as 'feminist' she reinforced their significance to people in general rather than women in particular.[38]

Of course, this notion of the 'individual' risks foreclosure on two fronts: first, on its convergence with notions of singular, artistic genius, and, second, on its reinforcement of the stereotype of Thai women artists being concerned with 'boring' personal [*suan tua*] issues rather than sociopolitical engagement.[39] Yet implicit in such warnings is a clear-cut distinction between individual and society, formulated as feminine and masculine domains, which might be alternatively constraining or liberating. Here, we might recall the potentialities registered in Araya's strategic replaying of the identificatory categories of 'Eastern' 'woman' in her installations and writings as a way of locating, within this confinement, possibilities of connection through the 'loving-kindness [*metta*] at the heart of that knot'.[40] Yet, clearly, this potential is not configured as found within a knowable, individual subject. Arnika Furhmann's understanding of Araya's address to the audiences of her videos as a '*performance* of feminine self-revelation' also applies here.[41] I would add to this that her installations posit the impossibility of knowing any 'self' beyond its production through readings that inevitably find their basis in public reception.[42] As evidenced by her reintegration of critical reactions to her practice into her later work, these readings might, in turn, be reread and re-signified in a nested process of formation and un-formation.[43]

This *mise en abyme* is well conceptualised in the artist's video installation *The Treachery of the Moon* (2012), in which she sits on a mat watching Thai soap operas on television with her dogs during their 'family time'.[44] Projected over the scene are news images of the 2010 protests led by the United Front for Democracy Against Dictatorship ('Red Shirts') and their suppression by the Thai military.[45] These images gradually submerge Araya and her dogs, eventually replacing the drama on the screen. The 'fictional' personal lives of the soap opera characters and the 'real' sociopolitical activities of the protestors both appear on public television, finding their reception in the private space

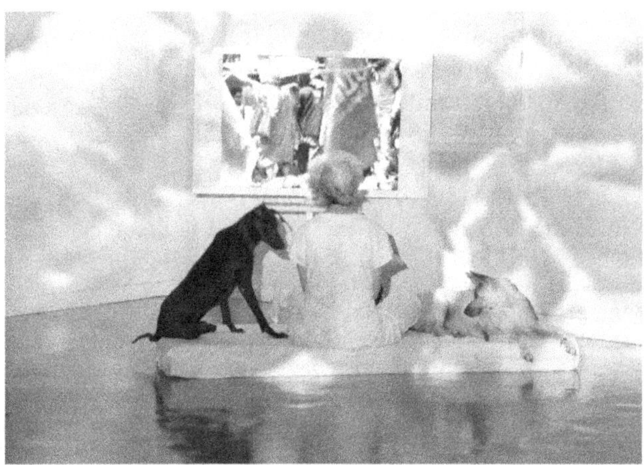

Figure 5.7 *Treachery of the Moon* (2012). Araya Rasdjarmrearnsook. Single-channel video. Courtesy of the artist and 100 Tonson Gallery, Bangkok.

of Araya's home. But this scene is then recorded and projected into the space of a gallery, where the images and their reception are read once more by another audience. The interpretations that we/she might bring to these public/private, personal/social images at once are culturally encoded and contain the possibility of 'joy, sometimes tears, sometimes anger' (Figure 5.7).[46]

Examining installation's fluid position in the stream of Araya's artistic career, within and beyond her focus on the medium in the early 1990s, again returns to the question of stasis and movement. For, in countering an understanding of this practice as a developmental stage, which was then superseded by more complex explorations of the relationships between art, life and death, it is not my intention to suggest that Araya's practice has remained stagnant. Rather, like the river, which rushes past but remains always in the same location, facilitating endless returns, reading Araya's installations from and within the perspective of her present practice yields differently sited conceptualisations of the ways in which they speak to and from the 'individual' and the 'social'. What is revealed is not the works' originary truth but rather the fluctuations of their stillness, produced through the process of reading. And through this, the artist and her work 'become a lake where a child bends over searching [for] what he really is. In me he is a young boy, in me he is an old man'.[47]

Acknowledgement

This text was originally published as Clare Veal, 'Water is Never Still: Araya Rasdjarmrearnsook's Sculptural and Installation Practice', *Afterall*, no. 47, Spring/Summer 2019.

Notes

1 This title draws from Araya's text, published to accompany her solo exhibition at the National Gallery, Bangkok in 1994. See, Araya Rasdjarmrearnsook, '*Nam Mai Ning* [Water Is Never Still]', in *Solo Exhibition* (exh. cat.), Bangkok: The National Gallery, 1994, np. I would like to thank Roger Nelson for his insightful comments on an earlier draft of this chapter.

2 For instance, Araya's installations have been analysed in conjunction with those of her former colleague at Chiang Mai University, Montien Boonma (1953–2000). See, for example, Leigh Toop, 'Installation Art from Thailand: Extending the Discourse on Installation Art', Unpublished doctoral thesis, Canberra: The Australian National University, 2009.

3 Examples of scholarly analyses of these works include Arnika Fuhrmann, *Ghostly Desires: Queer Sexuality and Vernacular Buddhism in Contemporary Thai Cinema*, Durham and London: Duke University Press, 2016,

pp. 164–165 and Sayan Daengklom, 'Waeo Siang Krading Kring Krung Khlung Klin Wa... "Chan Chue Araya" [A Faint Sound of Fragrant Poetry... "My Name is Araya"]', *Art Record*, vol. 9, no. 23, 2003, pp. 26–31. Partially republished in, *Araya Rasdjarmrearnsook: In This Circumstance, the Sole Object of Attention Should Be the Treachery of the Moon* (exh. cat.), Bangkok: ARDEL Gallery of Modern Art, 2009, np.

4 On the negative reactions to Araya's video works that deal with corpses, see A. Fuhrmann, *Ghostly Desires*, op. cit., p. 164.

5 See John Clark, 'The Thai Avant-Garde and Araya Rasdjarmrearnsook's Visual Work', in *Araya Rasdjarmrearnsook: Storytellers of the Town* (exh. cat.), Sydney: 4A Centre for Contemporary Asian Art, 2014, p. 15.

6 See May Adadol Ingawanij, 'Art's Potentiality Revisited: Araya Rasdjarmrearnsook's Late Style and Chiang Mai Social Installation', in David Teh and David Morris (eds.), *Artist-to-Artist: Independent Art Festivals in Chiang Mai 1992–98*, London: Afterall, 2018, p. 256.

7 For instance, D. Teh, *Thai Art: Currencies of the Contemporary*, Singapore: NUS Press, 2017, p. 154.

8 Ingawanij, 'Art's Potentiality Revisited', op. cit., p. 259.

9 My focus on questions of reading in this text is informed by a masterclass run by Ashley Thompson as part of the 'Gender in Southeast Asian Art Histories' symposium held at the University of Sydney, October 11–13, 2017.

10 Sayan Daengklom, as referenced in A. Fuhrmann, *Ghostly Desires*, op. cit., p. 171.

11 See Rasdjarmrearnsook, 'Rueang Nai Hong [Stories in Rooms]', in *Araya Rasdjarmrearnsook: Solo Exhibition* (exh. cat.), Bangkok: National Gallery Thailand, 1992, np.

12 Rasdjarmrearnsook, as quoted in Apinan Poshyananda, 'Araya Rasdjarmrearnsook: The Bitter Taste of a Private World', *Art and Asia Pacific*, vol. 2, no. 3, 1995, pp. 82–86.

13 See Helen Michaelsen, 'Traces of Memory: The Art of Araya Rasdjarmrearnsook' in Dinah Dysart and Hannah Fink (eds.), *Asian Women Artists*, Sydney: Craftsman House, 1996, p. 71.

14 Araya explains this in the interview, 'Araya Rasdjarmrearnsook: *Nam Mai Ning* [*Water Is Never Still*]', *Dichan*, vol. 19, no. 448, October 1995, p. 121. See also J. Clark, 'A Chronology of Araya Rasdjarmrearnsook', in *Araya Rasdjarmrearnsook: Storytellers of the Town*, op. cit., p. 123.

15 See, for example, L. Toop, 'Installation Art from Thailand', op. cit., p. 218.

16 See Rasdjarmrearnsook, '*Nam* [*Water*]', in *Phuying Tawanok* [*Women of the East*], Bangkok: Samanchon, 1993, pp. 57–65.

17 See Rasdjarmrearnsook, *Solo Exhibition* (exh. cat.), Bangkok: National Gallery, 1995, np. I first discussed these issues in Clare Veal, 'Can the Girl be a Thai Woman? Reading the Works of Araya Rasdjarmrearnsook from Feminist Perspectives', in *Araya Rasdjarmrearnsook: Storytellers of the Town*, op. cit., pp. 63–64.

18 See the interview, 'Araya Rasdjarmrearnsook: A Woman Who Has Her Affection for Death (The Female Artist Who Loves to Satirise and Irritate)' (trans. Judha Su and ed. J. Clark), in *Araya Rasdjarmrearnsook: Storytellers of the Town*, op. cit., pp. 116–117.

19 'Araya Rasdjarmrearnsook: *Nam Mai Ning* [*Water Is Never Still*]', op. cit., p. 123.

20 Curated by Apinan Poshyananda at the Asia Society and Queens Museum in New York City.

21 Lynne Cooke, 'Contemporary Art in Asia. New York', *The Burlington Magazine*, vol. 139, no. 1128, March 1997, p. 224.

22 Araya reflected on the physical reliance of objects on their supports in this work in an interview with Leigh Toop. Quoted in L. Toop, 'Installation Art from Thailand', op. cit., p. 212.

23 Araya recounts this in D. Teh and D. Morris (eds.), *Artist-to-Artist*, op. cit., p. 174.

24 In his review of 'Traditions/Tensions', Paisal Theerapongvisanuporn noted the emphasis on installations in the exhibition. See Paisal Theerapongvisanuporn, '*Muea Sinlapa Samaimai Khong Aesia Pai Kritkray Nai Niw York* [*When Contemporary Asian Art Struts to New York*]', *Hi-Class Magazine*, vol. 14, no. 157, May 1997, p. 108. Similarly, Patrick D. Flores has highlighted the significance of the 'installative' in the context of 'Chiang Mai Social Installation'. See Patrick D. Flores, 'A Changing World: Phases of the Installative in Southeast Asia', in D. Teh and D. Morris (eds.), *Artist-to-Artist*, op. cit., p. 278.

25 Julie Ewington, 'Five Elements: An Abbreviated Account of Installation Art in Southeast Asia', *Art AsiaPacific*, vol. 2, no. 1, 1995, pp. 108–115. See also the *Bangkok Post*'s review of 'Thai Tensions', a forerunner to 'Traditions/Tensions', which emphasised Northern Thailand as the 'source' of the materials used in *Buang*. Pattara Danutra, 'Commentary on the Modern Situation', *Bangkok Post: Outlook*, September 8, 1995, p. 34.

26 P. Flores, 'A Changing World', op. cit., p. 278.

27 Rasdjarmrearnsook, 'Interview with Araya Rasdjarmrearnsook, an Artist and Critic Based in Chiang Mai and Kamol Phaosawasdi Though Email and Fax, 15–30 March 2001', in *Dilemma: Kamol Phaosavasdi* (exh. cat.), Bangkok: Project 304 and Art Centre, Centers of Academic Resources, Chulalongkorn University, 2001, p. 44.

28 Ibid., p. 45.

29 Ingawanij, 'Art's Potentiality Revisited', op. cit., p. 262.

30 Ibid., p. 260.

31 Rasdjarmrearnsook, '*Sangkhom Suan Tua* [*Personal Society*]', in *(Phom) Pen Silapin* [*(I) am an Artist*], Bangkok: Samnak Phim Matichon, 2005, pp. 56–57.

32 On the non-applicability of 'Western' feminism to the work of Thai women artists see Somporn Rodboon, 'Issues of Thai Contemporary Women Artists', in Lee Weng Choy (ed.), *The 3rd ASEAN Workshop, Exhibition and Symposium on Aesthetics*, Singapore: ASEAN Committee on Culture and Information, 1995, pp. 122–123.

33 Christine V. McDonald and Jacques Derrida, 'Choreographies', *Diacritics*, vol. 12, no. 2, 1982, p. 68.

34 Rasdjarmrearnsook, '*Naenam Tua* [*Introducing Oneself*]', in *(Phom) Pen Silapin* [*(I) am an Artist*], op. cit., p. 24.

35 McDonald and Derrida, 'Choreographies', op. cit., pp. 69–70. This also has resonances with Ingawanij's extrapolations of the ways in which Araya's late style remains 'unreconciled with the present, figured as an indeterminate capacity to do and equally not do'. Ingawanij, 'Art's Potentiality Revisited', op. cit., p. 263.

36 '*Nam mai Ning* [*Water Is Never Still*]', op. cit., np, translation adjusted.
37 Ibid., np.
38 Theerapongvisanuporn, '*Ruprang Khwamkit Khong Khon Sinlapa Thangmot Chak Nitatsakan* Traditions/Tensions [*The Forms and Ideas of Every Artist in the Exhibition 'Traditions/Tensions'*]', *Sisan*, vol. 9, no. 3, January 1997, p. 38.
39 The risk that Araya's work may be interpreted in terms of '"western" gendered concepts of genius is pointed out in Brian Curtin, 'Queering Post-national Tendencies in Contemporary Art from Thailand', *Southeast of Now: Directions in Contemporary and Modern Art in Asia*, vol. 1, no. 2, October 2017, p. 138. Araya recalls a situation in which a visiting woman academic told her about the criticism she had heard from other (male) lecturers about Araya's work. As the visiting academic recounted, 'he said that Araya will never grow up. She makes art about her father, mother, grandfather and grandmother… It's boring'. See Araya, '*Sangkhom Suan Tua* [*Personal Society*]', op. cit., p. 59.
40 This phrase was used by Araya in response to a question about the ways in which her grandmother's experiences informed her understanding of relations between men and women. Araya, email conversation with J. Clark and C. Veal, October 2014. Similarly, in the catalogue for 'Thai Tensions', Araya related the 'specialness' of the individual artist to 'the way that he/she carries his/her heavy load, grasping to find connections and possessing fear'. Rasdjarmrearnsook, '*Buang* [*Trap*]' in *Thai Tensions* (exh. cat.), Bangkok: Art Center, Center of Academic Resouces, Chulalongkorn University, 1995, p. 9, translation adjusted.
41 A. Fuhrmann, *Ghostly Desires*, op. cit., p. 183, my italics.
42 I also anticipate that Theravada Buddhist notions of 'non-self' might play into this, although I do not have space to fully pursue that thread in this text.
43 See, for example, the video work *The Cruel* (2018), exhibited as part of 'An Artist is Trying to Return to "Being a Writer"' in which male students re-enact the various criticisms levied at Araya's work throughout her career.
44 The use of *mise en abyme* in Araya's installations and videos has also been identified in Ingawanij, 'Art's Potentiality Revisited', op. cit., p. 260. The description of this video as 'family time' is drawn from 'Artist Profile: Araya Rasdjarmrearnsook on "The Treachery of the Moon"', Guggenheim Museum, https://www.youtube.com/watch?v=xExZtNUJGHk (last accessed 5 December 2018).
45 The 2010 UDD protests were sparked by the Thai supreme court's decision to seize the frozen assets of former Prime Minister Thaksin Shinawatra. Thaksin's democratically elected government was ousted in a military coup in 2006. This was instigated following protests led by the People's Alliance for Democracy ('Yellow Shirts'), who claimed that Thaksin's government was corrupt and aimed to undermine the status of the Thai monarchy.
46 'Artist Profile: Araya Rasdjarmrearnsook on "The Treachery of the Moon" ', op. cit. John Clark has written about the relationship between the private and public in Araya's video practice from a different perspective than that outlined here. See J. Clark, *Asian Modernities: Chinese*

and Thai Art Compared, 1980 to 1999, Sydney: Power Publications, 2010, p. 118.

47 Rasdjarmrearnsook, 'In the Pool of Still Water There Is a Yearning for the Torrential Stream of the Big River', in *Araya Rasdjarmrearnsook: In This Circumstance*, op. cit., np, translator not credited.

References

Araya, R. (1993). *Phuying Tawanok [Women of the East]*. Bangkok: Samanchon.

Araya, R. (1995a). Araya Rasdjarmrearnsook: *Nam Mai Ning [Water Is Not Still]. Dichan, 19*(448), 115–128.

Araya, R. (1995b). *Solo Exhibition* (T. N. A. Gallery, Ed.). Bangkok: Amarin Publishing Center, Co. Ltd.

Araya, R. (2001). Interview with Araya Rasdjarmrearnsook, an artist and critic based in Chiang Mai and Kamol Phaosawasdi though email and fax, 15–30 March 2001. In *Dilemma: Kamol Phaosavasdi*. Bangkok: Project 304 and The Art Centre, Centers of Academic Resources, Chulalongkorn University.

Clark, J. (2010). *Asian Modernities: Chinese and Thai Art Compared, 1980 to 1999*. Sydney: Power Publications.

Clark, J. (2014). The Thai Avant-Garde and Araya Rasdjarmrearnsook's Visual Work. In J. Clark (Ed.), *Araya Rasdjarmrearnsook: Storytellers of the Town* (pp. 14–24). Sydney: 4A Centre for Contemporary Asian Art.

Cooke, L. (1997). Contemporary Art in Asia. New York. *The Burlington Magazine, 139*(1128), 223–224. Retrieved from http://www.jstor.org.ezproxy-al.library.usyd.edu.au/stable/887423.

Danutra, P. (1995, September 8). Commentary on the Modern Situation. *Bangkok Post: Outlook*, p. 34.

Ewington, J. (1995). Five Elements: An Abbreviated Account of Installation Art in Southeast Asia. *Art AsiaPacific*, *2*(1), 108–115.

Flores, P. D. (2018). A Changing World: Phases of the Installative in Southeast Asia. In D. Teh and D. Morris (Eds.), *Artist-to-Artist: Independent Art Festivals in Chiang Mai 1992–98* (pp. 264–278). London: Afterall.

Fuhrmann, A. (2016). *Ghostly Desires: Queer Sexuality and Vernacular Buddhism in Contemporary Thai Cinema*. Durham and London: Duke University Press.

Grounds, J. D. (1992). *Araya Rasdjarmrearnsook: Solo Exhibition* Bangkok: National Gallery Thailand.

Ingawanij, M. A. (2018). Art's Potentiality Revisited: Araya Rasdjarmrearnsook's Late Style and Chiang Mai Social Installation. In D. Teh and D. Morris (Eds.), *Artist-to-Artist: Independent Art Festivals in Chiang Mai 1992–98* (pp. 252–263). London: Afterall Books.

Lee, W. C. (Ed.). (1995). *The 3rd ASEAN Workshop, Exhibition and Symposium on Aesthetics*. Singapore: ASEAN Committee on Culture and Information.

McDonald, C. V. and Derrida, J. (1982). Choreographies. *Diacritics*, *12*(2), 66–76.

Michaelsen, H. (1996). Traces of Memory: The Art of Araya Rasdjarmrearnsook. In D. Dysart and H. Fink (Eds.), *Asian Women Artists* (pp. 68–77). Sydney: Craftsman House.

Poshyananda, A. (1995). *Thai Tensions*. Bangkok: The Art Center, Centers of Academic Resouces, Chulalongkorn University.

Rasdjarmrearnsook, A. (1993). *Phuying Tawanok [Women of the East]*. Bangkok: Samanchon.

Rasdjarmrearnsook, A. (1995a). Araya Rasdjarmrearnsook: *Nam Mai Ning [Water Is Not Still]*. *Dichan*, *19*(448), 115–128.

Rasdjarmrearnsook, A. (1995b). *Solo Exhibition* (T. N. A. Gallery, Ed.). Bangkok: Amarin Publishing Center, Co. Ltd.

Rasdjarmrearnsook, A. (2001). Interview with Araya Rasdjarmrearnsook, an artist and critic based in Chiang Mai and Kamol Phaosawasdi though email and fax, 15–30 March 2001. In *Dilemma: Kamol Phaosavasdi*. Bangkok: Project 304 and The Art Centre, Centers of Academic Resources, Chulalongkorn University.

Teh, D. (2017). *Thai Art: Currencies of the Contemporary*. Singapore: NUS Press.

Theerapongvisanuporn, P. (1997a). Muea Sinlapa Samaimai Khong Aesia Pai Kritkray Nai Niw York [When Contemporary Asian Art Struts to New York]. *Hi-Class Magazine*, *14*(157), 104–10.

Theerapongvisanuporn, P. (1997b). Ruprang Khwamkit Khong Khon Sinlapa Thangmot Chak Nitatsakan Traditions/Tensions [The Appearance of the Ideas of All the Artists from the Exhibition 'Traditions/Tensions']. *Sisan*, *9*(3), 35–38.

Toop, L. (2009). *Installation Art from Thailand: Extending the Discourse on Installation Art*. Canberra: The Australian National University.

6 *cellF*: embodying neural networks with musical bodies (Australia)

Darren Moore

In their 2006 paper "Towards a New Class of Being: The Extended Body", Oron Catts and Ionat Zurr put forward the classification of 'the extended body' to define the biomass of living cells and tissue cultivated outside of the body. This biomass is in the thousands of tons and yet does not fall under current biological or cultural classifications. The term addresses disassociated living cells and tissue by "re-examining current taxonomies and hierarchical perceptions of life" (2006, p. 1). It accommodates conceptual and artistic views regarding the implications of technologically augmented life. The 'extended body' also defines a growing body of work in the realm of biological art that uses biological material towards the creation of art. The *cellF* project is one example that uses in-vitro human neurons as the engine to drive a custom-made analogue modular synthesiser. *cellF* exists on the peripheries of art, science, music and design to create a semi-living musical instrument. It points the way to future scenarios of autonomous music-making entities that are driven by intelligence born from living cells and tissue.

What is *cellF*?

cellF is a collaborative project that brings together artists, scientists, musicians and designers to create the world's first neuron-driven synthesiser. It is a real-time interface between a cultured neural network and human musicians. It is an autonomous instrument that uses a neural network grown in-vitro as a 'brain' to control a custom-built analogue modular synthesiser 'body'. *cellF* defines itself through its use of biological 'wetware' as a control centre, focussing the project in a different direction than the current trend of technologically focussed artworks that use artificial intelligence 'software'. *cellF* portends a future in which natural intelligence-driven wetware-hardware hybrid entities will become more common (Bakkum et al., 2004; Potter, 2017) (Figure 6.1).

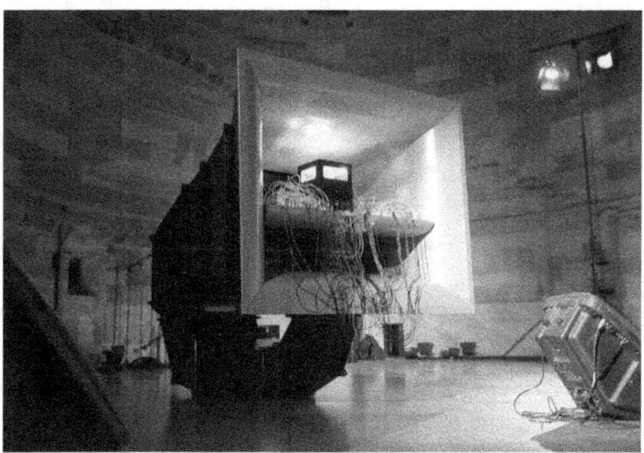

Figure 6.1 *cellF* at the Cell Block Theatre, Sydney, Australia. Photographer: Guy Ben-Ary.

The project was born from artist Guy Ben-Ary's love of music and a teenage dream of becoming a rock star. Instead of learning to play a musical instrument, Ben-Ary opted to create a biological alter ego. In 2012 he received a Fellowship from the Australia Council for the Arts to develop a biological self-portrait. The central tenet of his work is interfacing neural networks with technological interfaces; in other words, creating brains and giving them bodies. Ben-Ary is an artist that uses materials readily available to researchers in laboratories around the world and produces artworks that reflect on the future implications of these biotechnologies. He creates absurd scenarios that exist on the peripheries between living and non-living, highlighting not only what might happen in the future but what is happening now with existing technologies. Ben-Ary's work is collaborative and brings together artists and scientists to create works that upend the 'traditional' notion of what current biotechnologies can do. Ben-Ary collaborated with musician Darren Moore, artist Nathan Thompson and electrical engineer Andrew Fitch, along with scientists Stuart Hodgetts, Mike Edel and Douglas Bakkum, to develop the *cellF* project.

The brain

With cells as building blocks, *cellF*'s name derives from a play on the traditional artistic category: the '*cellF*-portrait'. *cellF*'s 'brain' is

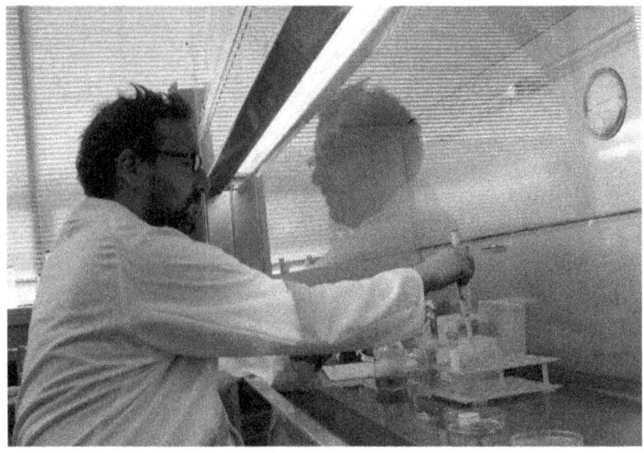

Figure 6.2 Ben-Ary in the laboratory in SymbioticA. Photographer: Guy Ben-Ary.

created using stem cell technology known as induced pluripotent stem cell or iPSC. Developed by Shinya Yamanaka and his research team at Kyoto University in 2006, iPSC works by programming the cell's genome into its embryonic state and transforming the cells into any other type of cell. Ben-Ary obtained skin cells from a biopsy of his arm tissue and sent them to Mike Edel at the Pluripotency Lab at the University of Barcelona; he, in turn, transformed them into embryonic stem cells and then neural stem cells. The neural stem cells were then frozen and shipped to Ben-Ary in Perth, where he differentiated the neural stem cells from neuron cultures at SymbioticA, situated in The University of Western Australia's School of Anatomy and Human Biology (Figure 6.2).

The artist research lab SymbioticA has been invaluable in the development of *cellF* and other biological art projects. Initiated by Oron Catts and Ionat Zurr in 2000, SymbioticA enables collaboration between artists and scientists, making it a unique environment in which to examine the implications of life from an artistic standpoint in state-of-the-art biological laboratories. This makes it possible for Ben-Ary and other bio-artists to develop a broad range of exploratory works.

Through trial and error, Ben-Ary developed a repeatable protocol for producing the neural networks used for each *cellF* performance. He starts several weeks before each performance to grow the neuronal cultures, culturing around 20 dishes. In the survival of the fittest, only the most robust and active cultures are chosen for the project. The neural networks are grown over a Multi-Electrode Array (MEA), which is a small dish with 60 electrodes that capture the activity of the neurons and can send electrical stimulations back to the network. The MEA acts as a read-and-write interface between Ben-Ary's external 'brain' with *cellF*'s synthesiser and collaborating musicians. *cellF*'s brain uses signals from musicians to induce changes in the neuronal structure, resulting in differences in the activity of the network. The range of activity varies from barrages caused by neurons firing en-masse to practically no activity at all. The project does not have scientific goals towards repeatable results or behaviours, and it is the unpredictability of the output that keeps the project interesting for the project team (Figure 6.3).

Human brains contain approximately 100 billion neurons, interconnected via trillions of synapses. *cellF*'s brain is symbolic as it only contains approximately 100,000 cells. Although a normal functioning human brain dwarfs *cellF*'s brain, its neural networks do produce a large amount of data in the form of action potentials and neuronal noise. The action potentials are used as raw material to produce sound.

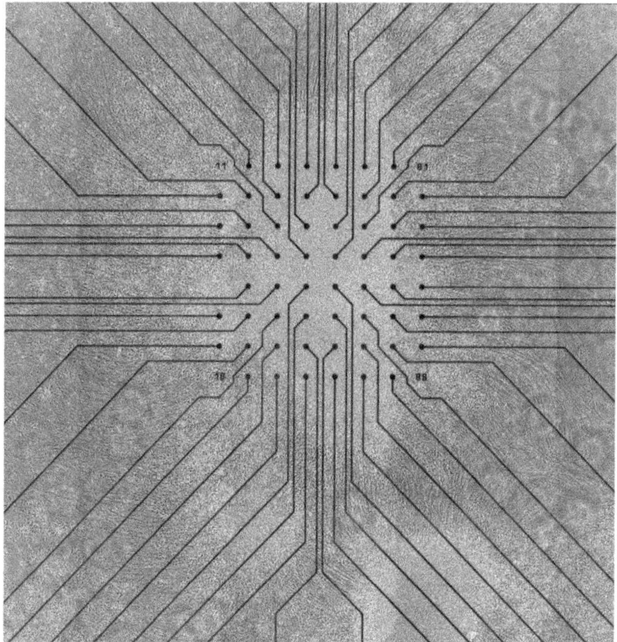

Figure 6.3 Multi-*MEART* electrode array used for *cellF*. Photographer: Guy Ben-Ary.

cellF's brain also responds to incoming stimuli from collaborating musicians and is subject to plasticity or structural changes. Plasticity is a term associated with learning in the brain, where neural structures change and adapt to new experiences. Whether or not *cellF*'s brain is learning and exhibiting emergent behaviour is outside the scope of this project. However, changes are occurring, which suggests that learning and adapting to new environments is a possibility. Additionally, the neuronal cultures have a lifespan and can only exist under strict laboratory conditions of 100% humidity, 37°C and carbon dioxide levels of 5%. The symbolism of the brain stands to entice the viewer to consider the future possibilities that these technologies present.

Embodiment

After successfully culturing neural networks from his skin cells, Ben-Ary began to consider options for the type of 'body' *cellF* should have. Ben-Ary's previous projects, *MEART* (2001) and *Silent Barrage* (2009), employed robotic bodies to translate the activity of cultured cells grown in-vitro (Ben-Ary 2014a, 2014b). *MEART, Silent Barrage* and *cellF* all share the objective of using neuronal data to perform artistic functions, albeit employing different methods. All three works explore the notion of the extended body and are artistic commentaries on the ramifications of new biotechnologies. They also use feedback loops to create parallels with human creative processes. *MEART* 'sees' by simulating visual feedback, *Silent Barrage* 'feels' by using spatial awareness and *cellF* 'hears' using sound as feedback. These methodologies point the way to future scenarios in which semi-living entities create autonomous artworks that process visual, auditory and spatial information in reaction to their environment (Figure 6.4).

MEART, the semi-living artist, uses a robotic drawing arm to create portraits. A webcam captures portraits of viewers in the gallery space and converts them into a stimulation map. The stimulation map uses information from pixelated photographs, sending the variations in colour intensity as electronic stimulation to the MEA housing a neural network grown from rat neurons. The information is sent via the internet to a neural network grown in the neuro-engineering lab at the Georgia Institute of Technology in Atlanta, USA. The neurons respond to the information/stimulations, and their response is then sent to *MEART's* drawing arm to create an interpretation of the photograph. The differences between the original portrait and *MEART's* portrait are then sent back to the lab as another stimulation map to create a feedback loop, which continues until the marks on the paper reach a certain threshold (Figure 6.5).

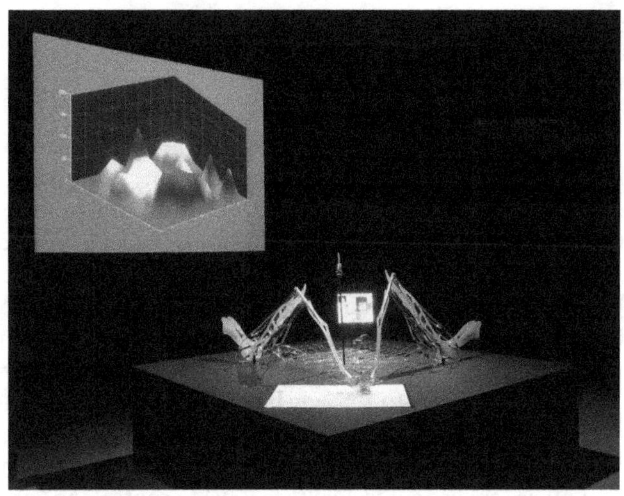

Figure 6.4 *MEART.* Photographer: Guy Ben-Ary.

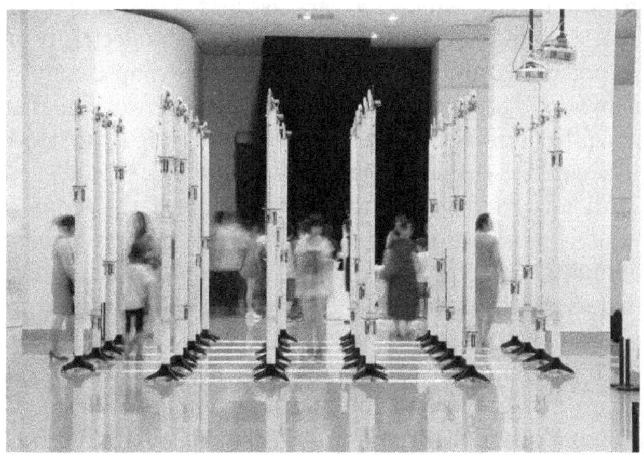

Figure 6.5 Silent Barrage. Photographer: Guy Ben-Ary.

Silent Barrage focussed on using robotics to translate activity from nerve cells. It is a visual spectacle of 32, 2.4-metre-tall poles placed around the gallery space, each with an autonomous robot. Each pole represents a region of a cultured MEA dish containing nerve cells. A rotating robotic pen moves up and down the pole, marking the activity from the nerves onto the poles in ink, serving as a symbolic 'memory' of the nerve activity. The work focusses on representing the uncontrolled activity of nerve tissue. Motion-sensing cameras capture information from audience movement, using them as stimulations for the nerve cells to create a real-time feedback loop. The result is a cacophonous scenario of autonomous robotic movement, reacting in real-time to audience movement.

cellF is a progression of the artistic ideas and methodologies employed in *MEART* and *Silent Barrage*. The meditation on the semi-living, the use of biological data and feedback loops feature prominently in all works. Ben-Ary built upon the foundations of his previous projects to develop *cellF*, arguably his most personal artistic vision to date. From the conception of the project, Ben-Ary wanted to create a musical 'body' for *cellF*. *MEART* and *Silent Barrage* produced sound as a by-product of robotic movement, leading Ben-Ary to consider robotics. However, using analogue modular synthesisers to embody Ben-Ary's in-vitro neural network was a more complimentary idea due to the way in which both the neural networks and the analogue modular synthesiser use electricity. Analogue modular synthesisers use control voltage (CV) to control the parameters of the synthesisers, with the different parts of the synthesiser connected via patch cables. The patch cables are what makes the synthesiser 'modular', with the ability to connect the various parts in near-infinite combinations. CV use in modular synthesisers represents the electricity produced by action potentials, and patch cables represent synapse connections in neural networks. The parallels in the way neural networks and analogue modular synthesisers use electricity made embodying Ben-Ary's external 'brain' in a synthesiser body an elegant solution.

The shift away from robotics in *cellF* turned the focus from an ocular-centric work to an aural-centric work. However, being born from robotic-focussed projects, *cellF* shares similarities with musical works that use robotics. Bretan and Weinberg define robotic musicianship as "the construction of machines capable of producing sound, analysing music, and generating music in such a way that allows them to showcase musicality and interact with human musicians" (2016, pp. 100–109). Although Bretan and Weinberg's definition of robotic musicianship describes *cellF*, it differs in several ways. *cellF* is not a humanoid figure trying to recreate the traits and idiosyncrasies of human musicians. Motion is essential to the production of acoustic sound, but with no moving parts creating sound, *cellF* cannot be judged against the rubrics of human musicianship in the way that other robotic musicians can. No visual stimuli also places the focus on listening as an essential element in the reception of the project.

What also differentiates *cellF* from conventional musical robotics is not its function but its process. Robotic musicians commonly employ software or artificial intelligence to identify higher-level musical features essential to human musical cognition. *cellF*, on the other hand, employs what Ben-Ary describes as 'in-vitro intelligence', which is an organic approach to cognition simulation. This type of intelligence stretches the boundaries of what can be considered intelligent. Post-performance feedback from the *cellF* team, audience members and collaborators suggest that the way *cellF* reacts to stimulations from its environment is similar to the unpredictable yet recognisable responses from improvising musicians. Why and how this occurs is not yet known, but perhaps it is the fact that organic processes are identifiable as human- or life-like. *cellF* is an experiment over a long time frame. It is an exploration of phenomenon that results from improvisatory encounters with various musicians and different environments.

cellF's body was designed by artist Nathan Thompson, who created an imposing sound-producing 'exoskeleton' that is at once practical and enticing to the viewer. The sculptural object contains analogue synthesisers, a bio-lab which holds *cellF*'s neural network as well as a class two sterile hood for maintaining and feeding the neuronal cultures. Thompson drew from the design aesthetics of the gramophone and the *intonarumori* or noise machines designed by Italian futurist Luigi Russolo. These two inventions not only influence the look of *cellF* but also acknowledge the importance of these machines to the development of electronic music, practically and conceptually. Practically, the gramophone ushered in the use of electricity in music; conceptually, the *intonarumori* embodies the emerging use of noise in music, as outlined in the 1913 *The Art of Noise: Futurist Manifesto.* The design was also informed by naturally occurring forms to form an endless internal loop as a metaphor for a closed-loop system. Like *cellF*'s synthesisers, the design is also modular so that it can be broken down and shipped for performances.

cellF's analogue modular synthesiser and neural interface were designed and constructed by electrical engineer Andrew Fitch. Fitch, who runs the Non-Linear Circuits synthesiser company, used existing designs as well as new modules custom-made for *cellF.* To represent neural processes, he employed feedback circuits, logic gates and chaos circuits alongside standard synthesiser components, such as oscillators, envelop generators, filters and amplifiers. All of the modules are controllable by the CV generated by the action potentials, giving the system the ability to produce sound autonomously. Fitch also designed the neural interface that connects the neural network with the synthesiser and improvising musicians. At the heart of this systems is the MEA dish that converts electrical signals from the neurons into

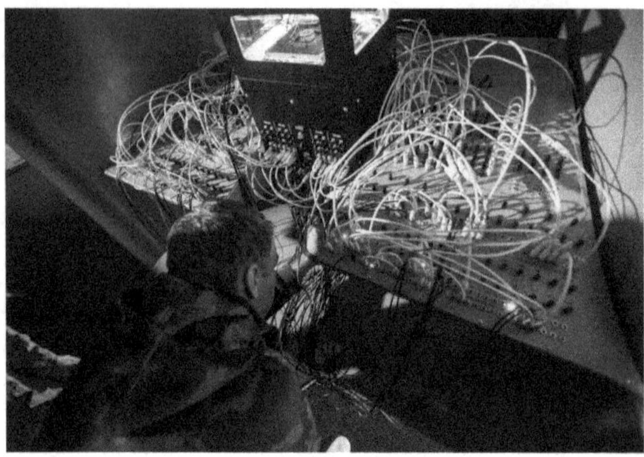

Figure 6.6 Moore calibrating *cellF* for performance. Photographer: Guy Ben-Ary.

CV and uses them to control the synthesiser and spatialise the sound via a matrix mixer. The matrix mixer sends the various patches of the synthesiser to 16 speakers placed around the periphery of the room. Also part of this system are frigates, which convert the incoming signal from the improvising musicians to electrical signals, which can then be fed back into the neural network, used to control the synthesiser or spatialize the sound (Figure 6.6).

During the developmental stage of the project, a software called NeuroRighter was used for digitising signals from the neurons and converting them to CV to interface with a prototype synthesiser. NeuroRighter was the primary interface for *MEART* and *Silent Barrage*, but Fitch realised that it was possible to build a hardware version of the interface to bypass the use of the software. As an experiential artwork and not an exercise in data analysis, it made little sense aesthetically or functionally to take an analogue signal from the neurons, digitise it and then convert it back to analogue again. Producing an analogue wetware-hardware hybrid helps to suspend the belief of the viewer that they are witnessing an autonomous semi-living entity. Works like *cellF* that utilise extended bodies displace humans as the auteur to became both the producer of the work and the work itself, producing a surrogate relationship between the donor of the cell line and the extended body. In *cellF*'s case, this relationship gives rise to the idea of surrogate musicianship, a term coined by the *cellF* team to describe the project. A surrogate musician produces musical content on behalf of the donor, with in-vitro intelligence becoming the control centre and source of creative output for the body.

cellF's development is not in opposition to robotic musicianship but an extension of this area where semi-living entities analyse and produce sound in response to their environment in real-time. The immediacy of electro-biological processes makes works like *cellF* suited to live performance situations and provides a platform to examine the inner workings of the creative process. The surrogate musician is the merging of the musician and the musical instruments to produce a new hybrid category of creative being. Also, surrogate musicians have the same cellular signature as their donors, offering artists the opportunity to be biologically linked to their creations in the ultimate form of personalisation. The concept of surrogate musicianship is only in its infancy, but *cellF* proposes fascinating possibilities of how music will be created in the future.

The live experience

cellF premiered at the 2015 Neo-Life Conference in Perth and has since featured at numerous international art and music festivals. *cellF* collaborates with improvising musicians in live performances lasting between 40 and 60 minutes. The first performance featured musical director Moore on drums, improvising with *cellF* to produce a post-human sound piece in front of an audience of approximately 150 people. Moore's primary role in the project is to patch the synthesiser to define the boundaries of the sound *cellF* will produce. *cellF* uses six to eight different patches to represent neuronal activity sonically while providing the scope for the sound to evolve organically. The aim is finding a mid-point between two states where differences in neuronal activity trigger sonic events. Moore draws upon his experience playing with *cellF* to guide new collaborators on what to expect (Figure 6.7).

Key to highlighting the autonomous nature of *cellF* is minimal to zero interference with *cellF* during performances. The premiere performance began with Moore fading in various patches of the *cellF* synthesiser before leaving it to run independently and moving to the drum set to begin the duo. The audience was silent as they witnessed a dialogue between Moore's reaction to the embodied neuronal cultures sonified and spatialised throughout the room, and the influence on *cellF* by Moore's drumming. The concert concluded with Moore standing up from the drums and approaching *cellF* to slowly fade out the synthesiser sound. In reflecting on performing with *cellF*, Moore had the following evaluation of the experience:

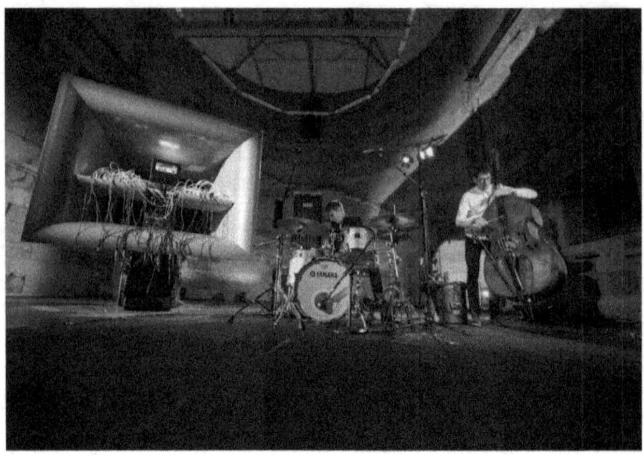

Figure 6.7 *cellF*, Darren Moore (drums) and Clayton Thomas (bass) performing at The Cell Block Theatre, Sydney, Australia. Photographer: Guy Ben-Ary.

> As a performer, I approached improvising with *cellF* in the same way that I would with another human musician. However, *cellF* behaved in a unique manner that was different to any previous performance I had encountered, so I decided to proceed slowly to let the sounds unfold rather than trying to dominate and force the situation. I chose to use a non-rhythmic, textural drumming approach using extended techniques. Firstly, because I thought it would provide a complementary sound palette to the abstract synthesiser sounds and secondly because I felt that abstract sounds contained less inherent meaning and are more open to interpretation. It was important that the focus of the performance was on the sounds themselves and highlighting the capabilities of *cellF* rather than creating a narrative.
>
> I felt the piece was well balanced compositionally regarding timbral variation, space, density and form. Whether or not I influenced this or if it was *cell*Fs behaviour is difficult to say. This was beyond my expectation as I was prepared for minimum interaction and unwieldy sounds from *cellF*. The sounds I produced were in reaction to the sounds I heard from cellF and it seemed like my sounds were affecting the behaviour and sound produced by *cellF* yet to what extent was hard to gauge from a one-off performance. I believe that with repeated performances, the behavioural tendencies of *cellF* will begin to unfold
>
> (Moore et al., 2016, p. 39).

Testimonies from attendees of the premiere performance highlight a clear cause and effect between *cellF* and Moore. Assessing the impact that Moore's stimulations had on the neural culture relied primarily on anecdotal evidence from the audience as there were no quantitative experiments performed during the development stage or performances. Perth-based musician and researcher Dr Adam Trainer, who attended the premiere, related the following observations about the performance in an email to the author on January 25, 2015:

> The first live outing of *cellF* in late 2015 arguably evidenced the conceptual validity of the project. Darren Moore's subtle and responsive playing treated the drum set not as a rhythmically-based instrument but as a textural one and was well matched to the modular synthesised noise that *cellF* emitted. Moore was able to gently coax an increasingly vibrant and responsive suite of textural electronics out of the network, using the occasion partly as an opportunity for improvisation, but also as a means of feeding the neural network so as to build the sound emanating from the synthesisers. Instead of careening wildly through stop-start percussive booms and crashes, Moore patiently encouraged and guided *cellF* through a series of restrained percussive approaches. This somewhat pensive improvisational approach paid off, with *cellF* responding gradually but with increasing certainty to the stimuli that it was fed. An encouraging start, perhaps, for what could potentially become an increasingly complex and multifaceted project
>
> (Moore et al., 2016, p. 40).

Although *cellF* can produce sound by itself in installation mode, it is the interfacing with human musicians that brings the work alive. It 'listens' to the improvising musicians by receiving electric signals summed from the musicians sound. It is the interplay between the improvising musician reacting to *cellF*'s sound and its receiving electrical stimulations from the musician's sound that defines the *cellF* experience. Witnessing it live is like being inside its brain. While *cellF* and improvising musicians are performing, the performance space transforms into a three-dimensional representation of the neuronal activity in *cellF*'s MEA dish. The action potentials generated by neuronal activity control an array of 16 speakers placed around the periphery of the performance space. At times the sounds from neuronal barrages can be violent and appear to spin around the room, and at other times, the activity is isolated and pensive. The experience for the listener changes depending on where they are in the room. The rhythm of the neuronal activity becomes palpable through sound and represents the complex web of interactivity in the neuronal culture.

Writer Jennifer Johung highlights the importance of the 'liveness' of a *cellF* performance in allowing viewers to hear Ben-Ary's cultured out-of-body neural network act and react in real time. Johung eloquently summarises the live *cellF* experience, stating that:

> ... our own differentiated bodies are placed in concert with the redifferentiation of Ben-Ary's cells and his reallocated *cellF* catalysing a variety of unforeseen collaborations across the micro and macro, living and non-living forms – from skin, neural, and embryonic stem cells to Ben-Ary and his host of art, science, engineering, and musical collaborators, from their bodies to ours, across biological lab, sterile hood, electrodes, neural interface, synthesiser, and sculptural form.
>
> (2019, pp. 134–136)

Conclusion

As Johung argues, perhaps the most significant implication of manipulating living and non-living matter with iPSC technologies is how it makes us rethink the forms and relations of how biological forms develop in and out of time (2019, p. 136). Ben-Ary's stem cells are cryogenically frozen, giving him the power to suspend and create life at intervals of his choosing. This act of creating new semi-living entities gives rise to a range of questions concerning what direction emergent biotechnologies will take us in the future. What are our responsibilities to these semi-living entities, and what kind of ethical boundaries need to be established? Artworks using biotechnologies elicit responses concerning shifting perceptions surrounding the understanding of 'life', particularly when natural biological processes are manipulated. By bringing possible scenarios to life, neural artworks confront the viewer, both instinctively and intellectually, by calling into question the liveliness of the differential categories of life and death, human and nonhuman.

cellF's journey, beginning with the culturing of neurons from skin cells through to the design of the synthesiser, interface and sculptural object, and subsequent live performances, demonstrates the ability to create wet-analogue surrogate musicians. This type of project is laden with possibilities. It challenges perceptions of how music can be made but also challenges the notion of what musicians and musical instruments are. The creation of musician-instrument hybrids directly linked through biotechnology suggests future scenarios where extended bodies controlled by in-vitro intelligence can transform the role of the artist. *cellF* is a thought-provoking work that highlights not only what the future holds but what is possible today.

References

Bakkum, D. J., Shkolnik, A. C., Ben-Ary, G., Gamblen, P., DeMarse, T. B., and Potter, S. M. (2004). Removing Some "A" from AI: Embodied Cultured Networks, in F. Iida, R. Pfeifer, L. Steels, and Y. Kuniyoshi (eds.), *Embodied Artificial Intelligence*. New York: Springer, pp. 130–145.

Ben-Ary, G. (2014a). *MEART*. Retrieved from http://guybenary.com/work/meart/

Ben-Ary, G. (2014b). *Silent Barrage*. Retrieved from http://guybenary.com/work/silent-barrage/, accessed June 21, 2019.

Bretan, M. and Weinberg, G. (2016). A Survey of Robotic Musicianship. *Communications of the ACM*, 59(5), 100–109.

Catts, O. and Zurr, I. (2006). The Extended Body: Towards a New Class of Being. *ISEA/Intelligent Agent Issue*. Intellect Press/Artnodes, ISSN 1695-5951.

Johung, J. (2019). *Vital Forms: Biological Art, Architecture, and the Dependencies of Life*. Minneapolis: University of Minnesota Press.

Moore, D., Ben-Ary, G., Fitch, A., Thompson, N., Bakkum, D., Hodgetts, S., and Morris, A. (2016). cellF: A Neuron-Driven Music Synthesiser for Real-Time Performance. *International Journal of Performance Arts and Digital Media*, 12(1), 31–43.

Potter, S. M. (2017). The Future of Computing and Neural Interfacing: Wetware-Hardware Hybrids, in *Future Now: Reconfiguring Reality* (M. Frauenfelder, B. Hamamoto, eds.), California: Institute for the Future, pp. 3, 57–59.

Russolo, Luigi. (1967). *The Art of Noises* (Futurist Manifesto, 1913). New York: Something Else Press.

Index

Note: *Italic* page numbers refer to figures and page numbers followed by "n" denote endnotes.

For Product Safety Concerns and Information please contact our EU representative GPSR@taylorandfrancis.com
Taylor & Francis Verlag GmbH, Kaufingerstraße 24, 80331 München, Germany

www.ingramcontent.com/pod-product-compliance
Lightning Source LLC
LaVergne TN
LVHW020639100826
845148LV00012B/2252

* 9 7 8 0 3 6 7 5 6 7 5 5 2 *